Pobal:

Seán MacRéamoinn

the columba press

the columba press

8 Lower Kilmacud Road, Blackrock, Co Dublin, Ireland

First edition 1986
Cover design by Bill Bolger
Typesetting by Typeform Ltd., Dublin
Printed in Ireland by
Criterion Press, Dublin

ISBN 0 948183 26 8

The publisher gratefully acknowledges the permission of the editor of *The Furrow* to use an edited version of Ben Kimmerling's article, first published in *The Furrow,* September 1986, under the title *Who speaks for the Laity?,* and of the editor of *Doctrine and Life* for *The Plain People of God* by Seán Mac Réamoinn, which first appeared in *Doctrine and Life* in October 1983.

Contents

Foreword:

This is, unashamedly, a book with a message, an exercise in propaganda. It is addressed chiefly, though not exclusively, to the Irish Catholic Laity, in order to alert their interest in the Synod of Bishops to be held in Rome towards the end of 1987. They and their fellows throughout the Church will be the subject of discussion: but it is to be feared that, as things stand, the voice of the laity itself will be heard only very indirectly, if at all. What is worse, the ideas and enactments of the Synod are unlikely to make any direct impact on ordinary Catholics.

Can anything be done about it? Some of us think an attempt should be made, first to get people thinking on the matter; secondly, to bring those interested together to express their beliefs and opinions; and, thirdly, to convey these to the Synodal fathers.

A small preliminary move was made in April 1986, when some fifty people from all over Ireland spent a day talking and listening and, finally, praying about it all. This was at the conference centre of Our Lady of Sion in Bellinter, Co. Meath. A synthesis of what was said, edited by a well-known religious journalist, is one of the core contributions to this volume, taking its place with a sheaf of essays by lay and clerical writers. A summary of the Vatican II document on the laity is appended.

Thus far our first step . . . *seo chuige in ainm Dé!*

A Holy Nation:
Laity and Ministry in the Bible

Sean Freyne

'All *the people* answered with one voice: all that the Lord has said we will do; we will obey'. (Ex 24:3)

'You are a chosen race, a royal priesthood, a holy nation, God's own *people.* (1 Pet 2:9)

To the authors of the Old and New Testament writings, our modern question about the role of the laity in the church, would hardly make sense. From the two quotations just given, one from each Testament, we can see how Israel and the early Christians undersood themselves before God — as a *people.* We find other expressions for this sense of collective identity scattered throughout the Bible: assembly; church; flock; community; body — these are the images that come most readily to mind. But whatever the word used, and whatever the circumstance of time or place, this sense of collectivity is everywhere basic to the Bible's understanding of the divine-human relationship. All else depends on and takes it meaning from that fact.

So it is very odd that the Greek word *laos,* meaning 'people', has given us the English word *laity* — as distinct from clergy: that a term which stood for the unity of all, now applies to only a part (in the eyes of some, the least important part) of God's people! The story of how that radical change of meaning has taken place is in a sense the story of the Christian Church in history — the gradual emergence of office in the Church, and the development of a legal understanding in which two orders — the clergy and the laity — became legal categories, each with its own status, rules and roles. The succeeding chapter will discuss this development in some detail.

There is an increasing awareness today that such a legalistic understanding of the Church is both pastorally counter-productive and theologically unsatisfactory. Vatican II, it is true, intended to restore the original biblical understanding, but with only partial success, it must be said. Developments since the Council have shown how resilient the old model has been, especially at local level. Both clergy and laity are ill-prepared to implement in a practical way the original biblical insight that God's people is primarily a collective unity, and that everything else, including ministry, is secondary to and in the service of that reality. Indeed it might be argued that the calling of a synod on the role of the laity shows that even Rome itself has not properly absorbed the image of the Church which the Council had sought to retrieve. It is highly desirable that there should be discussion on the practical implementation of the conciliar insights. However, in the light of recent events one is entitled to have reasonable suspicions that there is more afoot than merely pastoral planning. A reaffirmation of the juridical model of Church is high on the agenda of some at least of the more influential Roman voices which we have recently been hearing. It behoves the whole people of God to respond through the gift of the Spirit which it has received collectively at Pentecost, in order to assert again for our times that basic experience of 'being church' to which our biblical texts so clearly point. Here we shall focus on a few of the more important aspects, with an eye to current debates.

I. Why the Bible thinks collectively about our task
'A Kingdom of priests, a holy nation'

Why, one may ask, is this sense of collectivity so essential through the Bible? What insight does it offer on God's relationship with humankind? To answer such questions it must be remembered that the whole biblical story is based on the assumption that there is a fractured unity at the heart of the human situation. Though made good by God, humans, through their primordial ancestors, Adam and Eve, (themselves collective names for man and woman), lost their condition of blessedness. Such stories as the fratricidal hatred of Cain for Abel, the flood that destroyed the whole earth, and the tower of Babel, illustrating man's attempt to reach unaided the realm of God, all illustrate this underlying assumption that is at the heart of the biblical story. We have introduced, and indeed continue to introduce, into the human arena divisive forces that disrupt the intended harmony of the Creator for all his creation — with one another, with the created universe and with the global community of nations.

St Paul describes this self-destructing act as 'disobedience' (Rom 5:12-19) — a word that conjures up a rather paternalistic view of God. Yet it does help to direct our attention to the root cause of the problem, as the Bible sees it. By refusing to recognise that we are *creatures,* attempting instead to be Gods in our own rights, we have distorted not merely our relations with the living God but with one another also. Sin, in biblical terms, is both a personal *and* a social reality, and being justified (again to use a Pauline term, in the sense of 'being made right with God') means reconciliation and restoration of the lost harmony. The Hebrews had a very rich word to describe that restored condition, and the early Christians took it over and used it in their liturgical greetings. It is *shalom,* peace, meaning wholeness, completion and harmony. Ultimately it means blessedness.

With this simple, yet profound view of the possiblities and failures of human life, the bible could not but recognise that community-building, in the sense of shared life together, was at the heart of the reconciliation process. Thus the vision for Israel and for the first Christians was to become 'a kingdom of priests, a holy nation', because the Lord its God was holy (Ex 19:6; Lev 19:2), or, in the New Testament, to 'be perfect as the heavenly Father is perfect' (Mt 5:48). Unfortunately, both words, 'holiness' and 'perfection', are open to misunderstanding when taken out of the Biblical context. The one has overtones of an emotional type of piety whereas the other smacks of a stoical self-sufficiency. Both of these are wide of the mark.

The call to holiness implies worship. As a community of priests, recognising the otherness of God and celebrating his gracious presence with her, Israel is most truly herself — just as the creator had intended in summoning her out of Egypt. The call to perfection, which is equally a call to a radical following of Jesus (Mt 19:18) points to the moral dimensions of living. By answering the call both to holiness and to perfection in this sense, God's people restores the lost relationship with God and with one another.

For the early Christians, but also for the Old Testament people of God, these two calls are only different sides of the one process. Response to God in a worshipful recognition of his lordship also involved responding to his creation, particularly to one's fellow men and women within and without the community of faith. In practical terms this translated itself into concern and care for the needy — the orphans, widows and the poor. It is striking that both Testaments carry a clear condemnation of those who think they are worshipping God while at the same time neglecting the needs of those around them:

I hate, I spurn your feasts,
I take no pleasure in your solemnities;
Your cereal offerings I will not accept
But if you would offer me holocausts,
then let *justice* surge like water
and *goodness* like an unfailing stream. (Amos 5:21-24)

If, therefore, you offer your gift at the altar,
and there you remember your brother has anything
against you, leave there your offering before the altar,
and go first and be reconciled with your brother,
and then come and offer your gift. (Mt 5:23-24)

There can be no separating the love of God whom we do not see and the love of our neighbour whom we do see, as the author of the First Epistle of John reminds us (1 Jn 5:20). In that sense, both Judaism and Christianity are *incarnational* religions, not mystery cults. At their best both have to do with translating the religious meaning of life into a transforming force for this world. Right relations with God cannot co-exist with a distorted human situation. Again, it is typical of how concretely the Bible thinks of this distorted human condition that it repeatedly calls for *justice.* Right relations means a condition of *shalom* or wholeness which cannot be present in the midst of degrading poverty or tyrannical oppression. God's justice is biased and God's freedom is slanted — towards the poor and on behalf of the enslaved. It is only by co-operating with that justice and freedom that we can escape from the labyrinth of evil that we have cast around ourselves, making it impossible for us to escape from it by our own devices. It is a task that belongs to the whole human family, but believers have a special urgency in this regard since they consider that they have a profound insight into what is wrong, and the key to putting it right.

The role of the 'laity', in the modern sense of that term, is quite secondary, therefore, to the much more fundamental task of the vocation of *all God's people,* as seen by the Bible. It is only against such a background that we must now examine the insights the Bible has to offer on how best God's people should organise itself for its task. In particular what are the appropriate structures, what freedom of organisation is possible, and what flexibility is allowed to meet the changing circumstances of history and society?

II. Authority, responsibility, leadership.

The task of leading and directing God's people devolved from the start on certain central figures in several different roles. Thus, Moses is both prophet and priest, according to different traditions, and likewise, the patriarchs, Abraham, Isaac and Jacob can be readily depicted as offering sacrifices, as administering justice and as interpreting divine oracles for their followers. Gradually, however, the nation Israel developed political structures, similar to those of other nations —

13

specifically around the figure of the king, and, with this transition, there was a 'solidification' of religious roles also. In the sixth century BC, the prophet Jeremiah clearly evidences this development:

> The law shall not perish from the priest, nor counsel from the wise, nor the word from the prophet. (18:18)

Here, three separate types of religious leadership are envisaged — priest, scribe and prophet — and significantly, all three are seen as engaging in different forms of a ministry of the Word, with no explicit mention of cultic or ritual activity, as we might have expected. The specific roles of all three had developed further by the time of Jesus, when we meet scribes, prophets, priests, all with definite administrative roles in regard to the temple and the synagogue, the two great religious institutions of Jewish life.

Despite such developments, however, these varying forms of leadership never lost contact with the essentially collective nature of Israel's life — at least in the more ideal pictures. In practice, the priesthood in particular was in danger of becoming cut off as a caste apart, given the elaborate system of tithes and offerings that was devised for their material support, as they ministered in the temple of Jerusalem. Indeed, as time progressed, Jerusalem and its temple became the centre of activity of a whole range of officials, directly involved with the temple worship: priests, levites, cantors, woodcutters, incensemakers, those reponsible for correct slaughtering of animals etc. All these lived for and by the temple and were supported by the people who provided through their offerings for their material needs.

That being said, the belief that all Israel was a priestly people and therefore directly involved in worship never entirely waned. At the time of Jesus, groups such as the Pharisees and the Essenes are concrete evidence that many Jews felt that the overly structured priesthood and its Jerusalem ministry did not meet the real religious needs of the day. In that regard Jesus was not the only religious reformer within Judaism. The Pharisees devised a programme whereby the ordinary Israelite could live as a priest in the home and the village, thereby creating a direct link between the altar and the family table. The Essenes adopted an even more radical stance, declaring that their own community life constituted the proper form of priestly worship. Both groups can be properly said to have been protest movements, precisely because in their view the existing priesthood did not genuinely minister to the priestly vocation of all God's people. Though both groups adopted rigid lines of demarcation between themselves and outsiders, it is noteworthy that both put great emphasis on collective unity, rather than on any individual who might act on behalf of others.

Authoritative ministries of the word also existed in Israel. The prophet, the wise man and the scribe represent three different types of such activity. The first spoke more spontaneously, or charismatically, whereas the other two are based on tradition: the wise man was heir to a broad spectrum of general knowledge about life, acquired through experience, while the scribe was more a professional interpreter of other influential teachers' views. The fact that these varied ministries of word were separate from, and indeed sometimes antagonistic towards the priesthood, meant that there was already an important diversification of functions that has been largely lost in all the Christian churches today, especially in the Roman Catholic. Not only did these different types of ministry function independently of the priesthood, they also functioned against each other to some extent. In particular, the scribe and the prophet stood at different ends of the spectrum in mediating God's word to his people. The one spoke from his own authority based on God's call, the other from the authority of tradition; the one saw the immediacy of the current situation, the other was more concerned with loyalty to the past.

However, it is also important to recognise that, as with priesthood, the classic Old Testament writings saw the ministry of the word as a ministry to a people already

15

endowed with that word, at least in principle. In the Book of Numbers for example, Moses is represented as sharing his spirit with seventy elders, and he wishes that the whole people could prophesy (Num 11:21-29). In particular, the prophets of the restoration, Jeremiah and Ezechiel, view the situation of God's people of the end-time as one in which all will have God's word residing within them and be enabled through the gift of his Spirit to live up to its demands (Jer 31:31-34; Ezek 36:22-32).

It was into this Jewish world of differing perspectives as to how best to express the priestly vocation of God's people that Jesus was born, and amid these expectations about the prophetic nature of all Israel when messianic times would come, that he grew up. His community had no structure other than total acceptance of his word and a willingness to follow his call, with all its radical demands of service of the other, rather than the self. True, there was a permanent nucleus to this community, known as the Twelve. It was only later, after the resurrection, that the word 'apostle' became permanently attached to them, giving expression to the radical sense of mission to the world that was experienced by the early Christians. Jesus and his first followers saw themselves as representatives of the prophetic rather than the priestly strand of Israel's religious inheritance. Formal worship of the heavenly Father was not omitted but it was less important than the radical ethic of justice and love. The only pattern for ministry was the pattern of Jesus himself — giving himself on behalf of the other in love. Such service could not have its role defined in relation to other members, since it was the essential hallmark of the whole group.

During his life-time Jesus' community retained its unstructured and free spirit. Jesus himself was determined not to place any boundaries between the holy and the unholy, the priestly and the lay. All could share his banquet and there were no insiders. In particular, women were part of the permanent retinue of Jesus during his life-time (Lk 8:1-2), in direct defiance of those who observed the purity laws strictly. Women are said 'to minister' in his presence, and the significance of the Twelve was not that they were males but that they represented Israel's lost unity based on the twelve sons of Jacob. These aspects of his community were perceived as shocking by his contemporaries. The Pharisees and Essenes shared his concern to bring back collectivity to the centre of the stage but they were offended by his all-inclusive call to sinners and other socially (and religiously) unacceptable outsiders. Authority resided in Jesus himself but it was an authority based on the authenticity of his own claims of love and service, not on hereditary or other institutional grounds. It thereby negated the very structure of authority that was known in the Roman world of the day: 'among the gentiles those who exercise authority lord it over them; their great ones make their authority felt. But with you it will not be so' (Mk 10:42f). Henceforth, the exercise of authority in the Christian community was to be determined by the pattern of the cross, and that meant, or should mean, no self-seeking and no lording it over others.

Jesus' radical statement about the nature of the priestly people, in the name of claiming to call together the messianic people of Jewish hopes, inevitably meant that no clear blueprint emerged for authority and leadership in the early church. As we look at the different churches of the early days we see different patterns emerging – at Jerusalem, Antioch, Corinth, Galatia, Rome. For example, Paul, who had not known Jesus personally, developed the term 'apostle', in the sense of official representative, to express his own sense of what he was about. He also gave a theological interpretation to the variety of ministries that had emerged in the church at Corinth. All these are merely manifestations of the same Spirit, throbbing through the whole body of the Church. As long as they are used to build up the group and are controlled by the principle of love, they reflect the variety in unity that is a sign of the restoration of things, as they were in the beginning, which had now become possible through Christ (1 Cor 12-14).

Ministries differed according to local circumstances, it would seem. The lists that Paul provides at 1 Cor 12:7-11 and Rom 12:6-8 show a concern for the Christian liturgical assembly. But the very fact that they can vary in regard to the social circumstances indicates that there was nothing sacrosanct about any of them. It is remarkable, in view of our later history, that the term priest nowhere occurs. There were, presumably, leaders in eucharistic celebrations, and these were rooted in the apostolic sense of mission of Paul and others to re-present Jesus to local communities. Yet the very fact that nowhere is there any explicit reference to such leaders shows how relatively unimportant they were by comparison with the sense of unity that the eucharistic celebration engendered for all who partook in it (cf.1 Cor 10:16f; 14:20-25). Indeed our first pagan account of a Christian eucharist in Pliny's letter to the Emperor Trajan from Bithinia about the year 112 AD remarks on the sense of fellowship of the event through a meal and communal singing but does not observe on the presence of any particular leader, whom we might have expected to be mentioned in the interrogation.

As the early generations of apostles and other missionaries died, we can see emerging in the communities, of Paul in particular, permanent local leaders, variously called *presbyteroi* or elders, and *episkopoi* or overseers. The Church at the end of the first century and early in the second century was faced with many different interpretations, as the new faith came into contact with various philosophical and religious systems. The numbers of wandering preachers increased, often creating confusion and abusing the hospitality they received. As in all organisations, some structuring had to take place once the first fervour has died off. Key figures from the period of Jesus, whose witness could be traced back through the traditions of various churches emerged as authoritative now, in a way that was probably more accentuated than in their own life-time — Paul, Peter, James, John, for example. Influential local leaders such as Ignatius of Antioch and

Clement of Rome felt free to write to other churches about their internal difficulties. Yet, despite all these developments, nothing like the later divisions between clergy and laity had yet been formulated. Indeed, when by the middle of the second century the main-line Church was forced to draw up a list of authoritative documents as a rule of faith (the Canon of Scripture), this included Paul's letters, whose view of ministry ran counter to the later mood of institutionalisation that made such a list necessary.

It was in this way that a radically alternative view of the Church was kept alive, particularly with regard to the role of ministry. This vision would later function as a critique of a juridical understanding of office which divorced it from the body of the Church, thereby distorting the whole pattern of authority and leadership as envisaged by Jesus. This critique took its most radical (and tragic for the whole of Christianity) form at the 16th century Reformation. As the Roman Church at Vatican II has at last returned behind its canonical phase to its founding document, the Bible, it is to be hoped that the alternative image of itself that can be recovered there may help to heal the deep divisions of the past 450 years. If such a common witness to unity in diversity could be redisovered, then all the Christian churches, laity and ministers alike, might begin to bear witness to a world torn by divisions of all kinds, how it is possible to achieve the harmony of *shalom* — peace, that we profess to have achieved in Christ. It is an optimistic vision, given the present mood in the Church and the world, yet it is a vision we allow to disappear at our own peril and that of humanity as a whole. Within such an ecumenical vision of the Church the question of the role of the laity is indeed an important one, not however to establish their proper limits in relation to the clergy, but to insist that the original intentions of God for his people, as these were developed in Israel and re-defined by Jesus and his movement, be put into practice for the good of our world now.

Yet it might be fairly asked what implications all this has for church order today. Clearly, a biblical view not merely allows, but calls for a much greater diversification in ministry, with women playing a full and equal part at every level of the Church's life. The fact that the New Testament is reluctant to call any of the various ministers that emerged 'priests', suggests a critique of the existing situation as this was encountered in Judaism. Yet, as the office of priesthood emerged and was developed in the Church the model adopted was precisely that of the Old Testament priest – set apart from the people, with different rules and a separate life-style. (Here the Bible functions as a warning to us of how *not* to develop our ministry). Not only that, but this one office of priest now encompassed a variety of different ministries, especially those pertaining to the Word (preaching, teaching etc.), but also those of administration and ruling. Neither the Old nor the New Testament gives any warrant for such solidification of a variety of different ministries in the one office. In purely human terms these ministries call for rather different gifts. To expect any one person to have this combination of personal qualities often leads to frustration, or worse, cynicism in the ministry. We badly need to separate the ministries again and allow the rich variety of God's gifts in our communities to work together for the good of the whole – both in our liturgical gatherings and in our other social and ecclesial activities.

The question of variety of ministries leads on to an even more fundamental issue in the Church's life – the matter of different patterns of ministry in different Christian churches. Again, the Bible as a whole, but the New Testament in particular, can function as a powerful statement of protest against some of the on-going (seemingly endless) deliberations about validity of orders in different churches. In early Christianity both a hierarchical and a presbyterial (in the sense of a body of elders) pattern of ministry seems to have co-existed without any great theological problems being raised. A lot depended on whether the organisational pattern adopted by a local church was based on the household, the synagogue or the city. It is difficult to have patience with the 'dragging of feet' on this issue, and the more essential, but closely related issue of inter-communion, when one contrasts current practice, especially (but not exclusively) in Roman Catholicism, with the freedom of the Spirit among the early Christians. Such freedom does not mean anarchy, or that any and every form is either theologically or socially acceptable. What it does allow, however, is a genuine diversity based on social needs and cultural background. There is no easy blueprint for an adequate church order for our times. What the Bible offers and invites from us is that we would critically evaluate every spirit and yet take full responsibility for our freedom in Christ.

One Church: Two Classes?
The Lesson of History

Werner G. Jeanrond

As discussed earlier in this book all the Christian communities which together formed the early church understood themselves as followers of Christ and as proclaimers of God's salvation for this world. While expressed in certain (often different) forms and structures of organisation, all services in these communities were understood as functions of the one mission of the Church, namely to proclaim in word and deed the good news of God's presence in Jesus Christ.

When we compare the charismatic and spontaneous character of these early communities with the institutional character of the Roman Catholic Church today, we might easily be overcome by a nostalgic urge to return to such a church where all members listen to one another, where all services are seen in terms of function and not of status, where the gifts of the Holy Spirit are received openly and freely, and where, generally speaking, a Christian innocence prevails which we miss so much to-day. Yet — like all nostalgic journeys into the past — such a picture of 'original innocence' is pure illusion and projection. Because it is the very fact of tensions and problems even in those early Christian communities which gave rise to the institutional development of the Church. Therefore our historical retrospective is in no way an attempt to retrieve a past that never was.

Rather I would like to look at the development of our Church in the light of the theological criteria which we find in the New Testament. These texts are accepted as basic by all Christian communities; yet they need to be interpreted anew in any given time. Thus, we cannot hope to come to a once and for all definition of church organisation, but rather to find the framework in which every generation must decide if its church situation is still open for the spirit of Jesus Christ and for the fulfilment of God's promises. But first, we need to look at the historical development of the laity in our Church in order to see the necessities, opportunities, dangers and distortions which have been shaping this development — and which may be conditioning us similarly today.

So, in this chapter I would like to examine first the development of the two-class-system of clergy and laity in the Roman Catholic Church and question its legitimacy; I shall then reflect on recent lay-movements; and I shall conclude with a discussion of criteria for a more truly Christian organisation of our Church.

1. The Development of 'Laity'

As has been already pointed out, the early communities reflected in the New Testament texts only know one mission for the entire people of God. Of course, every community requires some kind of organisation, certain structures, in order to fulfil its mission. Thus, the earliest Christian churches already developed a number of specific ministries. Different people are graced with different gifts, yet, as Paul emphasises in 1 Cor 12, all are gifts of the one Spirit. Therefore, all the gifts and ministries in the community are of the same spiritual value and must complement one another; a particular gift must not be seen as calling for a particular status. However, the fact that Paul discusses this problem in his letter to the community in Corinth might suggest that the egalitarian self-understanding of the Christian community was already under threat. The threat increased with the development of an 'ontological' view of function and office in the community — that the member who bore it was granted a higher state of being than his brothers and sisters. We must ask what factors promoted this development?

The term 'lay-person' (*laikos* in Greek) appears for the first time in the year 96 AD in Clement's letter to the community in Corinth. Here the term refers to one of the 'ordinary faithful' as distinct from a deacon or a presbyter. However, it comes into general usage only in the third century, when particular structures of ministry are well established in all the Christian communities. The continuing differentiation of a threefold special ministry i.e. bishop, presbyter, deacon, during the first four centuries, had consequences more implicit than explicit for all those Christians who did not hold any particular office; they constituted the general body of the faithful. That, however, does not mean that they had no function in the ministerial organisation of the Church. Much, if not most, early missionary work was done by the normal working and travelling Christian. Christian women were responsible for most of the education of children in the faith, and all baptised faithful had functions in the liturgical life of the Church and in its organisation, e.g. the election of the community leader, the bishop. Yet, 'laity' emerged more and more as those who had no particular work or service — or were no longer allowed to have. Thus, the emergence of a 'laity' is the implicit result of the explicit development of clerical ministry. But because of the clergy's and especially the bishop's election by all the people, the two groups (clergy and laity) were in fact not separated from one another: leadership was an authority given by the community.

The early councils and synods confirmed the right and duty of the communities to elect their bishops, for only a properly elected bishop can truly represent his people to God. The ordination of the bishop by his fellow-bishops from neighbouring cities meant that he also represented God to his people, and stood in affirmed continuity with the tradition of the Church. Accordingly the bishop had two main functions: leading his particular community to God and proclaiming God's salvation to his community. He oversaw his presbyterial college and the deacons of his church. Such a clearcut distinction between bishop and presbyter was not yet common in the second century, but shortly emerged thereafter.

24

The new leader is then officially and visibly called to his ministerial functions through the laying on of hands in the act of ordination. This custom in the early church still points to the importance of the community as a whole. 'Absolute ordinations', that is ordinations outside a community, were theologically and ecclesiologically unthinkable for a long time, and were introduced only in the Middle Ages.

Generally, the leader of the community presided over the concelebration of the eucharist by the entire Christian community. The eucharist, then, used to be a celebration by the whole community; the priest or bishop led the community in the name of the community and with the authority bestowed on him through election by his people.

Christianity did not develop in a vacuum. Therefore it is not surprising that Jewish and Graeco-Roman images and organisational structures influenced the shape of the Christian churches. Particularly since the changes of the public status of the Church under Constantine, and most significantly under Theodosius, when Christianity became the state religion (381), the clergy increasingly adopted the rank and status of civil servants. In the aftermath of the Mass Migration and the conquest of the Western Roman Empire by the Barbarians, the Church remained the only functioning institution in that part of the world, and its clergy represented the only educated and influential group left. The philosophy of late antiquity fostered the 'ontological' distinctions, so that the clergy could begin to distinguish themselves no longer only through their function, but through their ordained 'being', from the rest of God's people. The notion of 'cultic' priesthood was adopted and further developed in the light of the spirituality created by the monastic movements, so that the clergy separated themselves still further from the general body of the faithful. The influence of the legal understanding of the medieval world completed this development. As in the feudal structure of medieval society, the Church is organised hierarchically (*hierarchy* means 'holy rule'). At the top of the hierachical pyramid we find the pope, and then the bishops, followed by the secular and monastic clergy, and, at the bottom of the pyramid, the mass of simple men (women did not count any more), the uneducated men of the world. The princes and rulers of the time were themselves sacrally anointed for their office, and therefore not really part of the laity. Thus, from the Middle Ages onwards, the Church was divided into two classes: clergy and lay-people. Moreover, the clergy were believed to realise God's commands completely whereas the lay-people could follow Christ incompletely. Therefore they are in need of total obedience to their perfect and powerful leaders. The spiritual perfection of the clergy eventually excluded marriage and demanded celibacy, thus widening the gap between ordained and non-ordained even further.

The changing understanding of the eucharist, from a community worship towards the ritual activity undertaken by an individual priest, went hand in hand with the development of the community leader to a ritualistic priest. It is no long the community that celebrates, but the priest alone, with the community now as mere spectators.

We cannot discuss here all the developments and dimensions of the medieval understanding of priesthood and laity. But the implications for the understanding of laity are now clearer: the ordinary believers are no longer an active force in the Christian Church, rather they had become *objects* of pastoral care administered by the ruling class of a ritually pure and legally defined hierarchy. The thus impoverished religious life of the laity found an alternative spirituality in the veneration of saints, the worship of relics, the crusades, and in a host of superstitious practices. Sometimes these alternative forms of spirituality were even organised for the laity by the clergy. A lively Christian community ceased to exist.

The complex history of the monastic movements cannot be discussed here. Yet the influence and encouragement which lay-people often found in these movements must not be underestimated. The monastic communities were, after all, still communities, and as such they kept something of the organisational initiatives of early Christianity.

The power of the medieval clergy and the intricate defence of its particular human, religious and administrative status on the one hand, and on the other, a laity reduced to a *function* of the clergy, make a radically different picture of church from the egalitarian image in the New Testament texts. In the earliest Church, ministry was a function of the people of God; now the people are a function of the ministry! In the earliest communities all gifts arise from the same Spirit; now only the clergy are thought to possess the Spirit in fullness. In the earliest Church the whole community celebrated the eucharist; now only the celibate priest celebrates while the faithful look on.

While some aspects of this medieval pattern have since changed, the basic structure of church, as organised *by* the clergy *for* the laity, has remained the official model in the Roman Catholic Church down to our own time.

One can hardly pinpoint a single fact or event which might have caused the self-understanding of the Church to develop in this particular way. And it would be wrong to say that mostly clerical ambition promoted the two-class-system of clergy and laity. Rather this development must be seen as a complex journey in which administrative practice and theological imagination slowly merged, helped further by the dynamic pressures of personal ambition. Nevertheless, it is remarkable to see how some of the most original theological and social insights and initiatives of early Christianity got lost, and how, ironically, many of the legal and cultic absolutes which Jesus had challenged slowly resurfaced and displayed a hitherto unknown power (e.g. the inquisition). The uncritical alliance and symbiosis between Church and State from the fourth century onwards provided the basis for this development of Christian self-understanding. And as long as the texts of the Bible were systematically withheld by the clergy from the laity, the basic Christian inspiration for

27

theological, ecclesiological and social change remained a closed book for most Christians.

2. The Lay Movement

To some extent the various monastic movements had been manifestations of protest against the clericalisation and the centralisation of power in the Church. Yet, the medieval papacy successfully integrated monasticism into its world, and sometimes even used it to foster its own power over against local bishops. The growing self-consciousness of the bourgeois class in medieval society also gave rise to some lay movements, but the official Church either integrated or expelled these.

As the Middle Ages came to an end, the Renaissance and the growth of humanism, the invention of printing, the discovery of new continents, the translation of the Bible into the vernacular, growing criticism of Roman triumphalism and misuse of power, and the political ambition of local princes, culminating in the 16th century Reformation, led to a significant lay movement. The priesthood of all believers was reestablished as the important biblical criterion for Church structure and the two-class-system of clergy and laity was theoretically rejected. Yet the confirmation of the special ministry of public proclamation and the administration of sacraments favoured, unintentionally, the actual superiority of theolgians in the reformed churches and the emergence of a new concept of laity. Now, lay people were characterised as theological illiterates, and therefore as dependent on the ordained minister. Hence the protest of the radical reformation movements, such as Anabaptists and Enthusiasts, who soon came to be persecuted by the new alliance of Church (now the Protestant Church) and State.

Within the Roman Catholic Church, the council of Trent did not change the overall understanding of ministry and laity, rather it strengthened ministerial power through the reform of clerical education. The subsequent development of the official Roman Catholic Church until the Second Vatican

Council is mostly dominated by an attempt to steer against political, social, philosophical and scientific movements in the modern world (e.g. Enlightenment, French Revolution, Industrial Revolution, Modernism, Marxism, evolutionary thinking etc.). Lay movements in the 19th century were either integrated into the hierarchical order or simply declared heretical. Lay movements were possible and welcome only if they 'participated in the apostolate of the hierarchy' (Catholic Action, 1922).

Nevertheless, the context within which the Church had to live had, despite the Roman Curia, changed irreversibly. The introduction of compulsory education in 19th century Europe and North America, the availability of the Bible in many languages, the development of democratic societies in the northern hemisphere, the ecumenical movement, the effect of the ambiguous role which the Vatican played in certain political conflicts (from pre-independent Ireland to Nazi Germany) led to a radical challenge of clerical authority and its complex defences. Moreover, the situation of the Church in a rapidly secularised world is again one of *diaspora,* so that clerical triumphalism has lost its attractiveness for lay people still willing to help build the church — not only for those who had given up already.

The Second Vatican Council eventually tackled many aspects of the new situation. In its statement on the laity it went as far as explicitly recognising the vocation of every baptised Christian to the apostolate of the Church. It emphasised diversity of service and unity of mission. Yet there can be no doubt that, according to this document, the clergy is in a special way charged with the ministry of the word and the sacraments. While lay people are encouraged to build the temporal order, their participation in the Church's ministry is defined solely by priests. The hierarchy is called to encourage the laity and a special secretariat for the lay apostolate is to be set up within the Vatican administration. In fact, the two-class-system and its theological defence, based on a 'special call' by the Holy Spirit, has not been changed at all.

Hence the Second Vatican Council did not alter the prerogatives of the clergy as the Church's ruling class. This is not surprising when one considers that the Council itself had no elected lay-representatives (nor did any of the subsequent Roman Synods). And many of the certainly well-intended promises of the Council's statement on the laity taste bitter in the light of a continuingly ruthless practice of appointing bishops, often against the will of the people (and in some places even of the priests), and with a view to restoring the threatened centralised order of the Church. Thus, in spite of the Council's encouraging affirmation of the common apostolate of all Christians, the deeply rooted medieval structure of hierarchy continues to exist. Educated lay-people are often mistrusted, particularly now that lay-people have access to the same education as clergy. Sometimes, the fact that lay Christians may be *better* educated than their clergy widens the gap which exists between the two groups even further.

Possibly the major challenge to the hierachical order of the Church today comes from women. Since the earliest days of the Christian movement women have been systematically excluded from many ministries and altogether from access to clerical ranks. All kinds of social, theological and metaphysical images have been used in the Church in order to legitimise the systematic ban on women from eucharistic ministries and from positions of leadership in the Church. For many men and women today, the recognition of this shocking attitude stimulates their call for radical change. Women were deemed to remain the eternal laity of the Church, while men had at least the chance to move up to a higher status. Over against the male-dominated structures of Graeco-Roman and subsequent societies, the Christian initiative of proclaiming the equality of all people as children of God had not been given a chance of success. One of the privileges of being alive today is to experience and participate in the change of consciousness in men and women with regard to the role of women in Christian communities. Yet a grave danger remains. It would be to miss a historic opportunity if one were to reduce the claims to a demand only for equal access to the ordained ministry. Rather, the feminist critique should help to unmask finally the inadequacy of the entire concept of ministry still operative in the Roman Catholic Church. The issue of the role of women in our Church is not only an issue for some active women; rather it must be the concern of all the people of God to work for change in the self-understanding of the Christian Church altogether.

The appreciation of the communitarian character of Church in the base-communities of South America and elsewhere has helped all Christians to rethink the mission of the Church and the necessity of working out more authentic structures. Everybody of good will will understand that the Church's call for justice in God's name lacks credibility as long as the same Church is itself unjustly structured.

Of course, many local communities within the Roman Catholic Church have changed radically for the better. But on the whole the originally medieval system remains in operation and keeps on distinguishing the very being of each male cleric from the lesser being of each of the faithful, and all that on the basis of an antiquated and highly questionable sacramental theology.

The question of the relationship between lay people and clergy is ultimately a question of the right understanding of church. As long as laity exists as distinct from clergy, authentic Christian community cannot come about. Thus, the lay movement's goal should be to dismantle the system of male-clerical dominance and work towards a new organisation of ministry in the Church. The truly Christian concern is to create a better Church in which the Spirit of Christ is given the freedom to call each member to her or his authentic contribution. What do we need today in order to facilitate such a church?

3. Towards a more authentic Church

The situation of the Roman Catholic Church today is

characterised by a serious crisis on a number of levels. The shortage of celibate clergy on the one hand and, on the other, the commonly perceived need for ordained ministers for the full realisation of Christian community has already led to a virtual collapse of church life in many countries. Priests are often reduced to the role of sacramental executives who tour many parishes in order to keep eucharistic celebrations going, thus promoting the separation between community and eucharistic leadership even further. This disastrous development, and the failure of any theological argument in favour of the conditions of maleness and of celibacy for ordination, have radically challenged the role and status of the priesthood today. And the Vatican's insistence on depriving local churches of their self-evident right and duty to appoint their own leaders has made most Roman dimensions of church government — good and bad — suspect. No curial or episcopal commitment to a renewed apostolate of lay people can conceal the basic Roman claim that only a clerical elite should possess ultimate authority over Christian communities and their organisation. What is needed is not just a strengthening of the laity by the clergy. What is needed is a radical transformation of our common understanding of 'Church' in the Roman Catholic Community.

This transformation must be informed by a discussion of the foundations of Church in the New Testament, and by critical insights into the social dynamic and the ambiguities of every human association. We need to ask whether the Roman Catholic Church to-day corresponds to what the New Testament has to say about any community wishing to follow Jesus Christ. Both our leaders and the community as a whole are always in danger of betraying our vocation. No evocation of tradition or succession can protect us from this danger. That is why any separation of the two groups in the Church is ultimately fatal for all. The community needs committed leaders so as to be protected from the tendency to confuse their ministry with an independently powerful status.

To be quite clear: ordination for certain ministerial functions is a richly meaningful mode of expressing our trust and prayer that God's Spirit may guide those whom we have appointed as our leaders. But is should never be misused to create a 'spiritual' elite which might claim immunity from the human dangers of distortion and betrayal. Ministry, ordained or not, must become an authentic function of the community, and the community must cease to be a mere object of its minister.

In order to create a more authentic Church, many aspects of our present structure and church life must change — and not only among the clergy. All must be willing and enabled to participate more fully. First of all, members must be willing to learn more about their faith, its biblical foundations and its historical development, in order to become able to assess their own situation more accurately. Then they would need to be willing to help to create a more lively local community. (It is shocking to see how few parishes in Ireland have parish councils, liturgy committees or the like. That is the fault of the laity, not of the clergy). Only active members can change community structures for the better. As long as the people in the Church prefer to 'keep their distance', with only an hour's presence on a Sunday, they do, in fact, support the two-class system of laity and clergy. When, however, a really active and committed local community establishes itself, it will bring its ministers more into the life of the community. Should the ordained ministers then refuse to cooperate responsibly with their people, their authority will be clearly in question.

This cooperation between the members of a church and its leaders should never be free from critical tensions. It is the task of the 'professional' leadership to serve the community critically and responsibly, and that will always lead to new challenges. It is the duty of the community to ensure that its leaders serve the community and not themselves. The unity of all local Christian communities and of the universal network of communities is the Spirit of Jesus Christ. Spiritual

33

unity, however, must not be equated with dull uniformity. The peace of Christ is not boredom, but includes respect for different opinions and approaches. The solution of conflict in the community demands humility, and a readiness to listen, so that every proposal can be assessed. The criterion for 'wrong' and 'right' is our common interpretation of the biblical texts and our faith in the God of Jesus Christ. This criterion does not necessarily call for identical organisation in every part of the world. But it certainly calls for a continuing dialogue and for increasing cooperation between all Christian communities. We all need one another; no one community is infallible. Together we can witness best to God's Spirit.

The vision of a more authentic Christian Church should not remain utopian or nostalgic. We all are called to follow Christ, and we all have received particular gifts to help in creating a truly Christian Church which could transform this world into a place reflecting its creator and his plans for for all of us. It is up to all the people of the Church to assume responsibility and spiritual authority, to create structures which facilitate such participation, and which transform the present two-class system into a more authentic, lively and loving community of Jesus Christ's people. There is no time or room for 'laity' in the sense of people who are alienated or detached and therefore not involved in this project. But there is room for every one who wishes to belong and to contribute to the people of God.

Important New Literature:

Edward Schillebeeckx, *The Church with a Human Face: A New and Expanded Theology of Ministry.* London: SCM, 1985.

Alexandre Faivre, *Les Laics aux Origines de l'Eglise.* Paris: Centurion, 1984.

Leo Karrer, "Laie/Klerus" in *Neues Handbuch theologischer Grundbegiffe.* Vol. 2. Ed. Peter Eicher. Munchen: Kosel, 1984. 363-374.

The Authority of the People:
Reflections on the Sensus Fidelium

Tom Stack

'In all times,' wrote John Henry Newman, 'the laity have been the measure of the Catholic Spirit; they saved the Irish Church three centuries ago, and they betrayed the Church of England.'

1.

Although rough-handled by Archbishop John McHale of Tuam during his Catholic university sojourn at Dublin (1851-58), Newman never fell out with Ireland. Though a figure of towering intellectual strength, the Oratorian Cardinal was notorious for his emotional fragility. I suspect then that the above 'bite at the hand that fed him' is partly, at least, intended as a thumbing of the Newman nose at his enemy, the ultra-montanist Manning, who had hurt him deeply. Be that as it may, the intellectual and religious education of the Catholic laity dominated Newman's apostolic enterprise from the time of his convension. This passion for lay development disquieted Rome and the English bishops of the time. Bishop Ullathorne is reported by Newman to have asked him somewhat sardonically on one occasion, 'Who are the laity?' To which Newman replied, 'The church would look foolish without them'. To Wisemen is attributed the patronising remark 'the only duty of the laity is to pay' (a slur, repeated in amplified form, but in irony, by Bishop Ernest Primeau at Vatican II, 'The laity are there to pray, pay and obey'). Most egregious of all was the 'jolly' remark of Monsignor Talbot, the English bishops' Roman agent at the time, and chamberlain to Pio Nono, 'The laity's province is to hunt, to shoot and to entertain'.

In modern times, the best known work on the activity of the laity in the question of doctrine is Newman's famous *Considerations on Consulting the Faithful in Matters of Doctrine.* In the course of this long essay (first published in 1833), Newman makes the following observations: Reference to the witness of the faithful is one of the preliminary requirements for a doctrinal proclamation. The testimony of apostolic tradition is entrusted to the whole Church in its various organs. The *consensus Fidelium* often replaces other theological sources. In the history of Arianism (4th century) he sees a prime example of the Church in a state, in which, to discover the tradition of the apostles, we must have recourse to the faithful. The 'divine dogma of our Lord's divinity was proclaimed, enforced, maintained and (humanly speaking) preserved far more by the *Ecclesia docta* . . . The body of the episcopate was unfaithful in its commission while the body of the laity was faithful to its baptism. The functions of the *Ecclesia docens* ceased for a time and it was largely the laity who defended orthodoxy.'

Newman's theory is developed in the preface to his *Via Media.* 'The vast body of the Catholic Church guided by the Spirit, is one, and from that oneness her various irreducible offices spring, conflicting with each other in pursuing their proper concern, but in this very act balancing one another, preserving one another from damaging excesses and joining together in one Divine centre. Church government, theology and pastoral experience have equal rights to raise their voice in the Church and have to come to concord in inevitable discord'.

What is the nature of this *consensus fidelium* in Newman? He describes it in five points:

(1) As a testimony to the fact of the apostolical dogma.
(2) As a sort of instinct deep in the bosom of the mystical body of Christ.
(3) As a direction of the Holy Ghost through baptism and the grace of faith.
(4) As an answer to prayer. In prayer it is not man alone who

is active as the one who asks in a spirit of faith, but God too, the invisible partner, speaks to the heart as the inner revealing teacher.

(5) As a jealousy of error which it (the *sensus fidei*) at once feels as a scandal. Here the supporting text from Aquinas is, I think, especially ad rem: 'Through the habit of faith, the human mind is inclined to assent to those (doctrines) which agree with the right faith and not the other ones'.

A study of the case histories of the proclamation of the dogmas of the Immaculate Conception (1854) and the Assumption (1950) show them both as telling us something of the *sensus fidelium,* this strand in Catholic tradition so painstakingly elaborated by Newman, but which seminally at least, goes right back to patristic times. It is found in, more especially, the authors of the second half of the 16th century who introduced the 'church universal' or the 'sense of the faithful' among the criteria of Christian thought.

The *sensus fidelium* lies within the *sensus ecclesiae.* These two terms, though distinguishable from one another, share a common basis which can be explained as follows: There is a gift of God (of the Holy Spirit) which relates to a twofold reality, objective and subjective, of faith *(fides quae creditur; fides qua creditur)* which is given to the hierarchy and the whole body of the faithful together and which ensures an indefectible faith to the Church.

In the cases of dogmatic definition mentioned above, it is clear that Pius IX and Pius XII have the explicit intention of doing nothing other than clarifying and fixing, by means of an official expression of 'definition', a belief already living in the consciousness of the people of God.

This is clear from Pius IX's encyclical letter of 1849 asking the world's bishops to inform him of the devotion of the clergy and faithful to the Immaculate Conception. In the bull of promulgation of this dogma, *Ineffabilis* (1854) it is the *perpetuus Ecclesie sensus* which is underlined. Likewise with regard to the Assumption, the same procedure and emphasis are recorded in the preliminary letter to the bishops *Deiparae Virginis* (1946) and in the bull *Munificentissimus* (1950). In the bull, Pius XII writes of the response to his earlier letter, which 'shows us both the concordant teaching of the ordinary magisterium of the Church and the concordant belief of the Christian people which the same magisterium sustains and directs'.

These papal formulae imply the linking, the convergence, of two great forces: on the one hand the spontaneous attitude of the faithful, and on the other hand the more explicit accord of the various leaders of the local churches (the joining of the *sensus fidelium* with the inclusive and more complete notion of *sensus ecclesiae*). To highlight the role of the *sensus fidelium,* especially in the case of the dogma of the Immaculate Conception, it is important to recall that the universal devotion of the people had, over the years, to establish itself in the teeth of stiff opposition from the anti-immaculist school of theologians as well as over the scepticism and indifference of a litany of popes.

Catholic life, existentially speaking, demands popular faith because of man's very nature. Tradition does not develop in linear fashion according to some mathematical formula. It progresses rather, through what I might almost call 'cultural moods'. It evolves through abandonments and enlightenments, by one step backward and two steps forward, by the recognition and declaration of the relative character of things which were long held, but which depended on cultural patterns which have now become part of the past. One may even wonder whether in the matter of 'defined' dogmatic points, a subsequent declaration on the same level of hierarchical authority might not place in a new and less important light what another age has expressed according to its own categories. Dogmatic progress does not primarily mean the addition of *truths* but the clarification of *the* truth.

It should be noted that 'popular faith' and 'popular religion' are not synonymous. This is so, quite simply, because faith and religion are distinct. This distinction has been thoroughly explored by Barth, Bonhoeffer and at a more popular level by Harvey Cox. Popular religion can be an entirely pre-rational expression of needs and emotions whose theological content may well be negligible. Speaking especially out of the Catholic tradition, however, it is worth recalling that faith, because it has to take hold of man as he is and all the roots that tie him to this world, does not stop at the intellectual acceptance of propositions and doctrinal tenets. Faith offers itself to the deeper self where it is embraced by the total personality of the recipient.

When we talk about 'popular faith' which is the prevailing characteristic of the two dogmas which we have discussed, we must draw attention to the danger of maximising, to the point of distortion, the role and agency of the *sensus fidelium.*

There is need for a dialogue between the various organs in the Church, a theological critique which takes place between the magisterium, the theologians and the *fideles.* An interplay between the three elements in clarifying truth is what the authentic life of tradition is about. In his early *De Veritate,* Aquinas included, among the effects of the gift of faith, the power of discerning teaching which was genuine from that which was false — even without instruction. This is obviously an over optimistic view. The history of the Church shows that at times, whole sections of 'simple faithful' have been drawn into error. But, by the same token, Church history reminds us that very often the mistaken notions, or willfullness, or both, of scholars and hierarchs have obscured the faith and sown error.

In effect, we may say that the magisterium functions, not as an authority added on to that of the Word of God, but rather as a service of discernment of what is being lived within the people of God on the very basis of their acceptance of the Word, in the 'power of the Spirit'. In other words, it is a service of guidance to the Church, as it incarnates in the world and in history the very word revealed in Jesus and passed on by the apostolic generation. The *instinctus,* the spiritual discernment, the religious needs, the true sense of direction of the body of the faithful carry the dynamism of faith where the Spirit wills; into the arena of humanity's search and sufferings, into its moments of triumph and failure, into its light and its shadows. In all this the magisterium acts in osmosis with the *sensus fidelium*. It is, in the language of electronics, forever wired for both reception and transmission.

2.

One way of examining the meaning of the *sensus fidelium* is by reviewing how Christianity was taught and transmitted from the earliest times. We find that the doctoral or teaching function within the Church developed as a prerogative of clerics and academics from a fairly early date. The unordained teacher, though never entirely absent, was a rarity.

In recent years however, the reflection of Christians on their lived experience, especially in what have become known as 'basic communities', is emerging more and more as a source of Christian insight, a body of witness which is forming a constituent of the living tradition within and through which Church teaching is expressed.

One can make a distinction between the authority of the entire believing community in the matter of faith, and that of the official Church. In other words, a distinction between the teaching *authority* of all and the teaching *office* of the few — those who have been given a mandate by the believing community, by virtue of the power of the Spirit dwelling in it, and in the name of Christ.

When Paul and Barnabbas were sent out to preach by the community of Antioch, the leaders there were 'prophets and teachers' *(didaskaloi)* (Acts 3:1-3). It is clear from documents up to and including the 3rd century that 'teachers of faith' could be ordained or non-ordained. They undoubtedly had great prestige in the Church. They had not been made teachers by a Church mandate. On the contrary they had become teachers on their own initiative on the basis of clearly recognisable gifts of the Spirit.

In the 3rd century Hippolytus refers to *doctores,* who were still either clergy or laymen. Origen was a great teacher while still a layman, but the clericalisation which had begun in Alexandria forced orders on what would seem to have been a reluctant candidate. Jerome too testifies to a lay 'doctorate'. However, the bishops had taken over all teaching by the middle of the third century, so that from then on there was simply a class of *sacerdotes doctores.*

It was not until the Middle Ages that a clear distinction reappeared between the 'teaching authority' of the 'doctores' and the 'teaching office' of the Pope and bishops. The latter were called the *Cathedra Pastoralis* whereas the former were known as the *Cathedra Magistralis.* Mediaeval theologians regarded themselves as *doctores* and as such were independent of the Church's authority. While these *doctores* were in fact priests, their teaching authority was not based on ordination or on a Church mandate. It was based on their university qualifications. (The prestige of the doctor Rector of e.g. the University of Paris was extraordinarily high; he took precedence over nuncios and cardinals).

But while the rise of the universities brought about the acceptance once more, of a non-official teaching office, nevertheless, by the same token, this development clearly narrowed down the 'universal authority of believers.' That universal teaching authority had in fact become the monopoly of an intellectual elite.

From the time of the French Revolution however, the doctoral caste lost its status. Since then it has been quite exceptional for lay people to make their own contribution to the illumination of faith by being called 'teachers of the Church', as in the case of Teresa of Avila and Catherine of Siena. The exception in this matter proves the rule. This recognition of exceptional figures does however point to what is somehow fundamentally present in all baptised persons; that is, a teaching authority in the Church outside the teaching office and the theological authority of scientifically trained men.

Since the Enlightenment, the notion of 'authority' has been recognised largely on the basis of intellectual knowledge and, partly as a result of this, the term *magisterium* has been reserved exclusively for the *official* authority in the Church, especially from the nineteenth century onwards.

Recently however we have come to recognise that the authority of reason has to subject itself to the criticism of the 'authority of suffering humanity'. If this does not take place, there is always a danger that leaders will come adrift, and this applies to both office-bearers and theologians. This is why the model of contemporary forms of liberation theology is so helpful and necessary: they express the implicit Christology and theology that exist in a people surrounded by suffering, and moved by a gospel impulse for the sake of their brothers and sisters. Suffering and patience in distress provide the basis for a memory of the Jesus Christ of the Bible and nourish a definite Christian praxis. A consensus comes about among those believers *who are the subject of their own expression of faith.* In this all that theologians do or should do, is to help them articulate their lived experience of faith.

In the past 'religious geniuses' influenced the consensus prevailing for long periods — Augustine, Athanasius, Thomas Aquinas and Luther. Now, however, we are at a new threshold. in addition to academic theology, there is also a theology of the 'basic group'. God's revelation is independent of people and their experiences, but it is, nonetheless, experienced by people, interpreted by them, and applied to the realities of their milieu.

Academic theology has the task of integrating the new experiences and the new praxis of local communities into the whole complex of the Church's memory, while at the same time, helping to prevent these new experiences from becoming intemperate, or divisive and self-defeating. In this way, academic theology 'mediates' the rich traditions of the centuries, down to its most localised life of today, and at the same time assists the particular churches towards that fellowship we call *koinonia.* And so a new 'zone' of the 'teaching authority of all believers' is being explored in our time.

The language of the teaching from 'the base' stresses human rights and dignity and the need to contest structural evil in unjust regimes. It is interesting how this emphasis links, in its origins, with the teaching of the official *magisterium*. The Justice and Peace thrust which seeded the dynamics of Medellin come from the teaching of John XXIII and Paul VI and the Roman Synod of 1971. (*Mater et Magistra, Pacem in Terris, Populorum Progressio, Octogesima Adveniens* and the phrase 'The work of Justice is a constitutive part of evangelisation' from the Synod). Medellin (as later, Pueblo) was, of course, a response not just to the theological reflexes of the Roman magisterium but, above all, to the *sensus fidelium* of the Christians of the Latin American sub-continent.

But the Church in the Philippines is also supplying the raw material for the development of doctrine from its struggle with oppressive social forces in this uniquely Catholic part of Asia. Two years ago the witness of an Irish Columban father, Niall O'Brien, made a spectacular contribution towards conscientising Catholics in Ireland and Britain on the Church's growing 'preferential option for the poor'. He represents a generation of Irish missionaries who are now returning, on rotation, from Third World countries and often immersing themselves in pastoral work in inner city Dublin parishes, and in other Irish urban centres. This 'reverse mission' is one of the more exciting developments on the Irish scene in recent years.

In Belfast for example, the Ballymurphy estate has, in its own way, all the credentials as a 'locus' for liberation theology. It is a community ravaged by the North of Ireland 'troubles', with many of its homes the victims of violence, touched by frequent deaths, imprisonment and massive unemployment. There also, the teaching Church is being made aware of the authority of the poor. Social conditions may not be identical with those of Latin America, but they are analagous, and represent a 'people of God' equally deprived. This 'authority of suffering humanity' has begun to find its way into the writings of theologians from the Irish missionary societies who match their writing with regular pastoral experience in Africa, Latin America, the Philippines and Ireland.

This testimony of the basic communities is being supported by academic theologians, following the teaching of insights of Vatican II (especially in *Lumen Gentium*). As a reflection of the *sensus fidelium* it cannot be ignored by the contemporary church.

Listen, please!
From Consultation to Dialogue

Ben Kimmerling

*As a Christian I am convinced that I and all other believers
are empowered by Christ. I not only believe this to be true, I
sometimes even experience it as true. I find this experience of
Christ's power and life exhilarating but not surprising — after
all it is what he promised would happen: 'I have come that
you may have life and have it more abundantly.'*

*So my feeling of 'What's the point? — my feeling of power-
lessness and lifelessness (because that is really what it is) — is
not to do with Christianity itself, rather it has to do with a
very particular aspect of my Chrisitianity — my relationship
with the official Church. The truth is that this relationship
frequently fails to mediate to me that abundant life which
Christ promised. Instead I often feel despairing, frustrated,
angry and blocked.*

*These life-diminishing feelings stem mainly from the
quality — or more precisely the inequality — of that relationship. As a lay person I have the impression that the official
leaders of the Church often speak for me and sometimes
at me but rarely or never with me.*

1.

To speak *with* implies relationship — it implies dialogue.
It is a two-way exchange. The dialogue is about stories —
two stories, not one, each told and each listened to. The
stories are about events; but just as important they are about
our feelings. We listen respectfully when Church leaders tell
us the story of salvation and of the Church itself. But I think
this story is incomplete and somewhat unbalanced because it
is a story told mainly by the clergy. We 'the faithful' need

45

now to be invited to tell our own story, the events of our lives and our feelings about them; and we need to be listened to by the Church leaders with the same respect that we give to them.

Only then will the laity begin to feel that basic equality of all Christians which is ours by virtue of our baptism. Only when this has been done, will a new way forward begin to emerge. For me at the moment there is a sharp contrast between the vision of that equality of all Christians, offered to me in the documents of Vatican II, and the real-life experiences of inequality which are part and parcel of my daily life as a lay person and as a woman within the Church. At times this provokes me to anger; but a more common and dangerous temptation is towards alienation and cynicism. I have to struggle very hard to prevent my feeling of anger and of being unheard from disrupting my relationship with the institutional Church — a relationship which I dearly want to preserve.

I often feel I struggle alone — or in the company only of other lay people, of a few understanding priests and of those sisters who accept that they really are lay people. The other partners in the relationship, other official Church leaders, seem to have little regard for such feelings. Perhaps in the past when blind obedience was considered a virtue, the feelings of the laity could be ignored with impunity. But in this psychology-centred age, when emotional honesty has become as important an aid in the search for truth as intellectual honesty, the feelings of the laity need to be taken seriously. The official Church needs to recognise that the Spirit addresses and challenges it through the anger and indignation of its people. If the official Church doesn't listen to the feelings of the people of God it will lose the emotional allegiance of its members. Already one can see this disaffection beginning to emerge in people in certain categories, e.g. the young, the unemployed, the under privileged of all kinds, married people, and women. In the Church's relationship with these people, a final breakdown is likely to come, not so much from an intellectual rejection of Christ's teaching as from a build-up of negative feelings resulting from being unheard. Unfortunately when breakdown does occur, the baby (the good news of Jesus Christ) will be thrown out with the bathwater (the unChristlike deafness and insensitivity of many Church leaders). In order to retain the loyalty of its lay members, the Church of today must be a sensitive and a listening Church.

What opportunities exist in the Church for lay people to tell their stories? What structure is the Church using to enable it to listen to its people?

2.

At the present time 'consultation' is the principal mode of listening used within the official Church. It is used by the higher ranks of clergy to consult the lower ranks, e.g. when episcopal appointments are being made. It is also being used just now by Church officials in order to listen to the laity. This is the consultation of the laity carried out by the bishops in preparation for the Synod on the Laity in 1987.

Consultation is a great step forward from unilateral decision-making. It helps to ensure that in the Church all the talking is not done by the leaders and all the listening by the faithful. Where those in authority are truly respectful and open, the process of consultation offers them the opportunity to hear the voice of lay people and to take account of it in their decisions. At its best it is like a hearing aid which enables Church leaders to tune in to the voices of ordinary Church members.

But a hearing aid can be used not only as an aid to hearing but also as a means of being selectively deaf. One can turn down the volume and tune out the voices one does not wish to hear. Have lay people good reason to place their trust in this particular 'hearing aid'? Now that they are being 'consulted' officially can they be sure that they really will be heard?

Consultation involves one party, on the invitation of the other, revealing his/her thoughts (and possibly feelings) on a particular issue. Thus the consulted party during the consultation reveals his/her true mind on the subject. In contrast to this it is not during the act of consultation but only after the ultimate decision has been handed down, that the true mind of the consultor is revealed. This procedure offers no guarantees that the opinions sought and offered will be either listened to or taken into account in the final decision. Neither does it provide an opportunity for come-back on a decision which proves to be unacceptable. It makes no promise of mutuality or Christian equality. It's a proce-dure where control is kept firmly in the hands of one of the parties.

The topic chosen, its scope, its focus, the degree of detail, the duration and timing of the consultation — all these are decided by the one doing the consultation. He/she decides who is to be consulted and, more significantly, who is not to be consulted — a comfortable arrangement for those who wish to remain deaf or who have already made up their minds! It is a procedure which is carried out on the initiative of the consultor. The consulted on the other hand plays a passive role prior to consultation and a passive role again afterwards. Even during consultation the freedom of the consulted to act is curtailed because, in order to participate at all, the conditions laid down by the consultor must be adhered to. In contrast to the consultor's freedom to *act,* the consulted party is only free to *react,* i.e. to accept or reject the invitation to participate and then to accept or reject the decision.

It is a procedure where decisions are made by some for others. The opinions of the consulted need not affect the lives of the consultor, but the decisions of the consultor, especially in the Church, often radically affect the lives of the consulted. When the decision is handed down, if it does not take the contributions or opinions of the consulted into account, no reason need be given for this ommission, nor need any explanation be offered as to how or why the final decision was arrived at. *There is no accountability.* It appears to involve a certain paternalism and superiority on one side and a submissiveness and inferiority on the other.

The consultative procedure then, while *permitting* the exercise of such values as trust, fairness, justice, respect for the dignity of others, openness, etc., certainly does not *safeguard or guarantee* them. Any assurance that these values will be respected depends, not on the structure itself, but on the magnamity, integrity and freedom from unworthy or unconscious motives of those who operate it. It also depends on a total trust in that integrity on the part of those consulted — a trust of a kind more usually rendered to God alone. Some questions necessarily arise here. Are Church officials entitled to this kind of trust? Have they in the past always proved worthy of it? Are they all fully mature and totally free from unconscious motivation or neurosis of any kind? Without this total integrity and maturity on one side and total trust on the other, the consultative procedure is open to abuse. It can be used either deliberately or unconsciously for the purpose of manipulation or control — activities which are incompatible with Christianity and which if present should give rise to indignation and righteous anger.

If decisions don't, on a fairly regular basis, reflect the views of those who have been consulted, then the consultative procedure is discredited and cynicism begins to creep in. A fairly obvious example of this is the cynicism of many priests about the consultation which preceded some recent episcopal appointments. Many felt that it would have been more honest of the authorities to dispense with consultation altogether and impose their own candidate. I have heard priests express the hope that some day (perhaps in the next appointment) the man who is offered a bishopric will state publicly that his acceptance of it is conditional on the majority of his priests agreeing to accept him. Certainly if this were an accepted custom consultation might become a more purposeful exercise.

Cynicism occurs when the consultative procedure is perceived as a cosmetic exercise — a hollow formality or ritual carried out to conform to the letter of the law — or as a sort of insurance policy or trump card which can be produced with a flourish when an unpopular decision is imposed. 'But you can't say you weren't consulted!'

What worries me as a lay observer of the clerical scene is that when priests feel themselves to be the victims of this type of consultation most of them seem to bury their righteous anger. One wonders whether this is done because of their total loyalty to authority or because there is no other real alternative open to them. Not only are their vocations as priests tied up with the institution but their livelihoods and legitimate ambitions are as well. Furthermore, they have reason to believe that if they protest they may be isolated by their fellow priests. In this situation their freedom to protest is effectively curtailed. Repression of righteous anger in our priests can result in an apathy and fatalism which is far from inspiring for the laity. Perhaps this is one area where the laity — whose livelihoods at least are usually not at stake (whatever about their reputations as loyal Church members) — could speak out their minds more openly in support of the clergy.

Even at its best this form of consultation can be a defusing device — especially, perhaps where lay consultation is concerned. Material which has to pass through various filters in order to be synthesised, loses most of its immediacy and passion. Human feeling is sieved out and only faint echoes of anger or dissatisfaction remain. Such sanitised material rarely makes compelling reading; it lacks impact and a sense of urgency. The material which is fed in may be sharp and piquant but almost inevitably what emerges is bland and insipid. What goes in as dynamite comes out as blancmange!

I think that it should be noted also that it makes a considerable difference who synthesises the material. Inevitably if men synthesise the submissions of women, or middle-class people synthesise those of the poor, or celibates those of the married or bishops and priests those of the laity, the decision as to what is of importance in the original submission is left in the hands of 'outsiders'. The possibility therefore of bias inevitably creeps in — a bias based on the status or sex or class of those who make the synthesis.

In the 2000 years of Church history women have rarely been allowed or encouraged to contribute their insights to the development of theology or Church laws. It remains the same today. By being excluded from the ministerial priesthood women are also being systematically excluded from the decision-making level of the institutional Church.

A similar difficulty arises when celibate clergy set out to articulate a theology of sexuality for married people. The recent pastoral *Love Is For Life* has much to recommend it. But I want to illustrate my point by quoting from one of its key paragraphs (par. 9):

> Sexual union says 'I love you . . . I need you, I can't live without you . . .'

I take it that the bishops here are presenting to us married people what they see as the ideal; for it is only too obvious that sexual union in practice does not often say this. But is it a true ideal? If so what of the man whose wife died suddenly yesterday? Has he for years been saying to her 'I cannot live without you.' *Should* he have been saying that? If so what can one say to him now?

I think it is simply wrong to teach that one who 'makes love' is saying or ought to be saying 'I cannot live without you.' I believe rather that the ideal of married loves includes some peripheral awareness of the fragility of life. The ideal is not 'I cannot live without you' but rather 'Our present union enables me to live life more fully now and will continue to strengthen me even if some day I have to live without you.'

My point is that in the passages I quoted we married people are being asked to live our lives according to a theology that does not reflect the full reality of our lived experience. We are in danger of contorting our relationships in our efforts to conform. If we fail to fit the pattern we are made to feel guilty. Alternatively, if we remain true to our experience we may feel obliged to reject the whole theology and the institutional Church as well.

I am not denying the hierarchy's right and duty to issue pastorals on marriage and sexuality but I think such documents would be more acceptable – and probably more readable – if married people could speak for themselves in parts of them. Such documents would be enriched by the reflections of married couples on their lived experience of marriage in the light of Christ's teaching. Similarly Church teaching on sexuality would be enriched by the insights of women into the meaning of human sexuality. So long as such documents are written by the hierarchy after limited consultation only, there is no opportunity to challenge what is said in them until the document is already in circulation. Those who want to challenge parts of them then are trapped. If they speak out they may be seen as disloyal but if they remain silent they allow Church teaching to become remote from the lived reality and therefore less relevant to those it aims to help.

Consultation for the purpose of compiling synodal documents or pastoral letters does not adequately serve the needs of the laity – a laity which is not a homogeneous mass, but is made up of many disparate groups each with distinct needs – needs which only they themselves can know. Consultation provides no real opportunity for our spiritual leaders to hear the authentic voices of these groups – to put on record the stories of these people. These stories, if justice is to be done to them, must be told, not by remote others at second and third hand in sanitised words and phrases (we all know how boring and distorted third-hand stories can be). They must be living stories told at first hand in the authentic voice of the people themselves. Even soap powder ads recognise that it is the authentic voice of Mrs X which is most likely to sell the product. Can the leaders of the Church then, as they have been asked by the gospels, not be as wise in their generation as the children of this world and find a way of letting people speak for themselves?

If consultation is inadequate what's the alternative? The only one that I can suggest is dialogue. It is a way that offers both sides the possibility of a satisfactory outcome, that respects the basic equality of all Christians and that allows all parties to move forward together in unity.

To move from consultation to dialogue would involve change — radical change — in attitudes and in structures. If our leaders are to allow us to speak for ourselves they must be open to that change. They must have a sense not only of the past but of a new and exciting future too; not just a taste for history but a taste for science fiction as well! An ability to contemplate with equanimity a Church of the future which will have changed almost, but not quite, out of all recognition, to meet the unknown needs of a new generation. However, in order to be open to the future the Church must first of all be genuinely open to the present, to the here-and-now needs of its own members — the unemployed, the handicapped, the married, the single, the poor, the old, women — and men too. It must dialogue with them all.

The call to dialogue is a call to understanding, a call to respect, a call to a recognition of the basic equality of all Christians. It means that leaders who listen must be free enough, unthreatened enough, and confident enough in their God, to let the whole story pour out — the frustrations as well as the achievements, the anger as well as the joy, the nasty bits as well as the nice bits. Only in the kind of mutual trust that allows us all to tell our story — the story of the whole Church as it really is — can there be any hope of real encounter. The call to be available, to listen, is a call to a new, a more challenging, perhaps a more painful but also a more honest way of being together. And — who knows? — in travelling this way together we may find that place that the bishops have been called upon by the Synod document to find: 'a place — primarily a spiritual place and more than just a material place' — a place 'of encounter and dialogue'.

Women:
Part of the Laity?

Margaret MacCurtain OP

So much has been written about women by women in the decades since the *Decree on the Laity* in 1964 that it is tempting to take the reader on a grand tour beginning with Mary Daly's *The Church and the Second Sex* and Rosemary Haughton's *On Trying to be Human*. With Rosemary Radford Ruether, these are probably still the most widely read and influential women theologians: moreover they are laywomen, two of them married and mothers of children. It is just possible that Vatican Two has made them indispensable, not just to the general reader but to the professional churchman or woman who is wise enough to recognise the rich content of their faith-explorations.

The last two decades have been a harvest time of feminist thought and scholarship within the Christian disciplines, a phenomenon quite unprecedented before the present century, though having its roots far back in the primitive church as Elisabeth Schussler Fiorenza has demonstrated in her widely-acclaimed biblical study, *In Memory of Her* (1983). To understand the U-turn that women have accomplished in their perception of their status within the Church, no more salutary exercise is recommended than that of reading the *Concilium* volume in the series 'Religion in the Eighties': *Women, Invisible in Church and Theology* (1985). In the concluding editorial reflection, Professor Mary Collins, OSB remarks: 'women are suddenly to be found visibly present and persistently vocal in great numbers in centres of theological reflection both in Europe and North America and in assemblies of local churches everywhere. These women are asking new questions and questioning old answers'. Professor

Collins points out that the World Council of Churches encourages theological reflection by women: the Roman Catholic and Orthodox women remain outside the official activity of the Church of Christ even as they continue to minister everywhere a Christian liturgy is celebrated. Her conclusions are, on balance, optimistic but she warns church leaders: 'Christian women in India and all of Asia, Africa, and Latin America are only slowly making their ways to the hall of study. Women of the first and third worlds are just beginning to find one another in a new network of Christian sisterhood and feminist reflection'.

In many personal ways the late twentieth century has been one which has given women an open sesame to education, to waged work, child welfare, trade union protection and political participation. And women are living much longer than ever before: child-bearing and women's health have benefited from the fact that women have become active as nurses, doctors and pharmacists. What is startlingly different about the end of the twentieth century is the manner in which women are seeking to control their own destiny, be it biological, or economic. Women are now convinced that they can contribute actively to the government of the planet. Traditional mind-sets expressed in aphorisms like 'the hand that rocks the cradle rules the world', and 'behind every great man is his mother' have been loosened. Family stereotypes have been brought into question, or silently discarded and a great-grandmother is rarely now described as someone's 'relict'.

From another angle, one that affects humankind at its deepest level of survival, the twentieth has not been the greatest of centuries. It has been a time of spiritual darkness for western civilisation. It has seen two world wars, as well as the Jewish Holocaust, forcing Christians to ask fundamental questions about the nature of our beliefs (or prejudices). Despite a United Nations Charter, it has been a cruel century for children to be born into because of hunger and homelessness. Over the third millenium which approaches swiftly there is a dark threat of nuclear destruction. Mass pollution from radiation hangs over planet earth, so fair to look at from a space-craft, and the prospect of star-wars is no longer science-fiction.

Yet for women it has been *the* century where they have gained entry into the real world of paid work, of knowing how to acquire information, which is always a significant threshold for the powerless to cross. They are deemed capable of running a borough or a country, through the democratic process of the vote. For the first time, civil law has permitted women to limit their families scientifically, and has allowed them the choice of marriage or non-marriage without social or political stigma. In short it has been a great century of freedom for women — though not for all women.

Almost a hundred years ago Matilda Joslyn Gage, an American religious thinker linked freedom for women with the act of speaking out their minds. 'The most important struggle in the history of the Church is that of women for liberty and thought, and the right to give that thought to the world'. Any genuine change in the public perception of women's position in society is inextricably bound up with changes in language. A study of words that have come widely into dictionary use in the seventies include *machismo, male chauvinism, sexism.* All are now accredited dictionary words and there exists a substantial body of international directives issued by librarians requesting that official documents endeavour to avoid terminology which perpetuates sex stereotypes. Once a concept has been embodied in a word, we can begin to accept or reject the symbol. Language always expresses the effort to break out of cultural moulds of the past, even as it strives to formulate newly-sensed alternatives. Nearly two decades after the word *sexism* entered fully into English usage and acquired its status, most women and many men have become aware of how deeply ingrained the thing itself is in western culture. Probably coined on the analogy of *racism.* they are both 'sixties' words.

But it was Rosemary Radford Ruether's *Sexism and God-Talk* published in 1983 that established what was tantamount to a new set of principles of Christian theology. In a closely argued text she covers practically all theological topics being discussed in this decade and it is difficult to escape from her inexorable logic. 'If all language for God/ess is analogy, if taking a particular human image literally is idolatry, then male language for the divine must lose its privileged place. If God/ess is not the creator and validator of the existing hierarchical social order, but rather one that liberates us from it, who opens up a new community of equals, then language about God/ess drawn from kingship and hierarchical power must lose its privileged place'. Boldly she goes on to declare: 'feminists must question the over-reliance of Christianity, especially modern bourgeois Christianity, on the model of God/ess as parent'.

To Mary Daly the essential mental exercise is 'to hear our own words always giving prior attention to our own experience, never letting prefabricated theory have authority over us'. This was the position she held when she wrote *Beyond God the Father* in 1973. For her the power of meaning is an important step in focusing reality afresh. Reclaiming the power of *naming* brings a new meaning context to our spiritual consciousness: 'words that, materially speaking, are identical with the old become new in a semantic context that emerges from qualitatively new experience'. For instance the images of women that permeate the religious consciousness of the Christian west, woman as temptress, the Eternal Eve, the gateway to hell, and their polarised opposites, woman as virgin, pure and undefiled guardian of the hearth and home, constrain the real person in a strait-jacket of good and evil. If religious experience is to continue to be meaningful for women, with their newly-developed self-awareness, then a 'cultural and religious heritage which continues to assure that man sets the standard and is the norm for being human' is at odds with the search to name the new theological models which are needed to define the contemporary world, and interpret the religious metaphors afresh. Daly rejects the Judaeo-Christian tradition in favour of a world-view based on women's experience. Ruether's self-admitted premises are a Christian paradigm, and for her, at this time, feminist theology is a restatement, which removes the male from his central role, thus ultimately clearing the way for a liberation theology for women. For both, language and naming hold the key to this new awareness.

When women, in the early seventies, began to challenge the adequacy of masculine language for expressing the attributes of God, they were not advocating an application to God of 'femininity' as a way of countering past prejudices. They were studying the contemporary translations of Bible, Missal and Breviary into the vernaculars and voiced a collective dissatisfaction with a language unliberated from what a group of women theologians identified as 'the dead hand of sexist theology'. Language not alone expresses experience, it conditions it. Metaphor as a means of shorthand, a swift recording of a complex inner experience thus demands scrutiny. An examination of religious metaphors in translations of the Bible yielded evidence that *power* metaphors play a significant part in mediating the nature of religious experience. The noun forms are preferred to the verb in describing images of power, for example the word *king* where *ruling* would give a more accurate meaning. The verb being a more dynamic form of expression allows 'stretch', and the possibility of additional meaning.

If bias along the lines of gender is built into the English language, as it is in most of the vernacular languages of western Europe, what then is the nature of the dominant culture that has cast communication into such a mould? The global community is heir to a culture which is a civilisation in a true sense but one that harboured colonisation, slavery and militarism. It has always placed a premium on peace through a precarious balance of power which in turn has necessitated war and armies. It has given to the world a system of economy, based on property and profit-making, but often at the expense of the powerless. And its evolution has been underpinned by *patriarchy.*

It is important that we see patriarchy as Aristotle did: a system of governing human beings, founded on the relationship between governors and governed, in the state and in the household. For him patriarchy was founded on 'nature', and as a corollary 'marriage was the union of natural ruler and natural subject'. Slaves, as well as women, were not 'fit to rule'. The freeborn Greek male head of the household owned and disposed of wives, children, slaves and property: he alone had the right to full citizenship. Scholars have noted the contradiction between the ideals of democracy, and the actual unequal social structure reflected in the system of government, the central legacy of Athenian democracy to the world. All are not born free.

Language – nouns, verbs and pronouns – are the reality in which human beings communicate. The prevalence of masculine nouns and pronouns in the English vernacular version of the Latin Breviary, issued in 1974, and given an imprimatur that approved its use for Australia, England, Wales, Ireland, New Zealand and Scotland gave to many of its women users a sense of being excluded. Nor was the American version which followed any more inclusive, despite the growing awareness of sexist language among American women religious. The use of 'sons of God', 'God of our Fathers', 'my brothers', 'the God of Abraham, Isaac, and Jacob', or versicles such as 'he who thus serves Christ is acceptable to God and approved by men' did little to reassure women that they were an integral section of the People of God. The intercessions which round off Morning and Evening Prayer of the Church were even more blunt in their use of the masculine. Take Monday, Week Three, for Evening Prayer, in Part One of the Breviary, and the reader finds the response: 'Draw all men to yourself' in answer to such intercessions as: 'The will of Christ is for all men to be saved. Let us pray that his will may be done'. More frequently the reader comes across intercessions like: 'Let us pray to Christ the Lord, the

59

sun who enlightens all men, whose light will never fail us'. The list could go on. . .

Patriarchy carried over from the Athenian political system to Christianity, and dominated the earlier call to discipleship in Christ towards the end of the first century AD. It was a gradual process of adaptation by Christianity to the pressures of Graeco-Roman society and modes of government.

The patriarchal model of church, thus understood historically, underpins much of the reality of the Church in the world. Its public government is one of male hierarchy, and its authority as the Church of Christ, viewed from outside, looks like a pyramid with jurisdiction, and obedience to that jurisdiction, essential to its structure. The sixteenth-century Reformation did not transform the patriarchal ecclesial model, it merely replaced the medieval clerical elite with the family whose head was the father, and in the new world the egalitarian aspects of the Radical or Anabaptist Reformation got submerged in the powerful coalescence of capitalism and colonialism.

For women in the Church the reality of their experience is not a comfortable one. They have no part in the clerical elite that rules them yet as laypeople they receive their definition by way of differentiation from the cleric. Yves Congar's pioneering study in the early fifties, *Lay People in the Church* (1957), gave the needed impetus to those engaged in determining the place of the laity in the Catholic Church. Previously, lay people of the calibre of Frank Duff and Edel Quinn had a promoted a lay form of spirituality and Catholic action that paralleled the twentieth century missionary movement, and they had won the support of bishops and clergy, notably that of Cardinal Suenens, one of the great thinkers behind the emergence of the role of the laity in Vatican Two. Another form of lay-presence at the heart of the Church's mission to the poorest was the person and work of Dorothy Day in the United States. A third type of lay-involvement had emerged in Australia through the activity of Maisie Ward and Frank Sheed.

What Congar was drawing attention to in his splendid study was the inescapable logic that followed from the primary distinction between the layman and the cleric, or between the lay-state and the clerical state. It is, he insists, that distinction which defines the layman, or the laity. His work was an endeavour 'to fill the space between', and his conclusions are embedded in the *Decree on the Laity*. The avowed purpose of his book he declared was: 'to study the sacred state of the christian laity, first in its constitution as a whole, and then in the detail of its substance'. Rosemary Haughton in *The Catholic Thing* (1979) also explores 'the space between': 'among the reasons for writing a book of this kind is the need to discern the development in ideas about what on earth the word "Catholic" symbolises now, in minds that entertain it'. Her people include Baron von Hugel, Augustine of Hippo, Heloise, Edmund Campion, Erasmus, Dorothy Day and Peter Maurin. She then looks at a representative group who for her illustrate the 'radical tradition' within the Catholic enterprise, and in particular the French lay philosophers who clustered around Jacques Maritain, or came after him.

Neither Congar nor Haughton address themselves specifically to the question of the laywoman's definition or status. To eyes sharpened to notice sexist language, Congar's *Lay People in the Church* uses the masculine noun and pronoun unvaryingly and the more generic term, 'laity'. It seems to the writer now that Yves Congar, that most ecumenical and perceptive of theologians, was actually signalling the reality, that women were part of the laity, but not lay women. Rosemary Haughton whose infallible ear has picked up the distress that women are experiencing about their position is, in the eighties, addressing this problem and bringing to it her unique gifts of discernment.

The eighties are a plateau-stage for women. When the new Code of Canon law was promulgated in 1983, one distinguished lay woman in the Vatican commented: 'at least it has given us the status of laity'. The development of the concept of the laity which Congar explored historically was a gradual process, and roughly paralleled the growth of western monasticism. Both became 'states' in the Church viewed as institution. At the end of the first century AD the lay person was the husband of one wife. In the second and third centuries the term lay people was reserved for the male administration and the payer of tithes to the bishop. Congar, in determining the role and function of the laity, remarks: 'the Code (of Canon Law) is not the place to look for an adequate answer to questions about the laity'. The verdict of history demonstrates that the canonical status is a determining one in defining the lay person. Only in 1983 does the new Code grant woman a recognised status. She is now a lay person in her own right!

In the Latin Breviary there was a curious category among the common offices at the back of the breviary, abbreviated to 'nec . . . nec' *('neither a virgin nor a martyr')*. From this common office were drawn the elements for the celebration of the feast of a married woman saint. Traditionally the Church has always been slow in raising lay, and married, women 'to the altars of the Church', a phrase full of sacred symbolism. The virgin on the other hand has occupied a particular protected position in the Church's liturgy and in canon law, and her reappearance in the new Code, in Canon 604, as the 'order' of virgins has implications beyond this essay's scope. Women's total exclusion from ordination in the new Code is a kind of apartheid which sets them apart from their male lay counterparts who can still choose the clerical or lay state. A woman has not that choice. Leaving aside the issue of women's ordination, it is a salutary exercise to reflect on what precisely the new Code permits women to perform. Many women must have realised over the last few years that the homily is expressly reserved to the priest and deacon, and that if they read liturgical texts, or act as servers or acolytes at the altar, they do so by the goodwill of the local bishop or parish priest. If the present theology and interpretation of the 1983 Code so wish, women can be excluded from liturgical or church ministries.

Equally serious, at a time when women have enjoyed the benefits of unversity education for well over a century, is their almost total absence from accredited theological faculties. Canon 819 provides for the education of young people, clergy and religious, but there is no specific recommendation concerning women. That means, in practice, that women are back to the early days of seeking university degree accreditation, with its accompanying hazards of financial outlay and the fear of non-recognition at the end. Even if that obstacle is surmounted — and an increasing number of women are studying theology and endeavouring to take their doctorates in theology — there is no guarantee that women will be hired by theological faculties, much less get promoted to senior positions. It would be interesting to ascertain how many such senior posts are occupied by women theologians at major seminaries or Catholic universities. The full implications of the 1983 Code have yet to be experienced, and the complete equality expressed in Canon 208 beckons like light at the end of a very long tunnel.

There is a text in Luke 13 which shines out in the setting of salvation history. It is the healing by Jesus in the synagogue of the woman bent double for eighteen years, 'possessed by a spirit that crippled her'. When Jesus healed her, 'at once she straightened up and glorified God'. It is salvific for women to know that she considered praising God far more important than breaking the rule that a woman should not be heard in church. When Rosemary Radford Ruether visited Dublin in 1986 she addressed a large gathering of women, lay as well as religious. 'Men', she said in one of her asides, 'decide that what we are asking for is a slice of the cake, whereas what we are really demanding is a new recipe'.

Fifty Voices:
A report From Bellinter

Kevin O'Kelly

The fifty men and women who gathered at Bellinter came from all over the country. They were of widely different backgrounds — rural, urban, inner city, suburban. They worked in schools and factories, in offices and kitchens, and on the land. Half a dozen were under twenty-five, most under forty-five and a few over sixty. Their commitment to the task in hand, to the prospect of the Synod and how an Irish lay voice might reach it, was clear from the fact that they nearly all had travelled long distances to talk and listen and learn. They had no pretensions of being 'representative' of the Catholic Church in Ireland, but in their different ways, they all belonged . . . They shared many hopes and fears and doubts. They did not claim to have the answers. But they asked each other many questions. Kevin O'Kelly was listening.

Is the Church truly on mission to the world? Does it really see the Spirit working there? If the Spirit is working in the world why is the Church apparently so afraid of that world? Why does it urge the need for protection against the 'world', 'the media' and 'secularisation', when its own people are helping to shape that world through political action, and the results are mediated through the secular media?

Nobody seemed to think present church structures were much help in trying to accomplish its mission. Even so, the talk during the day was usually cheerful. The Spirit was working in his people — wasn't he? The kingdom *would* come. At the same time, there were frequent irritated interruptions deploring ecclesiastical structures and attitudes that seemed to get in the way of the kingdom rather than help its coming.

Many had themselves experienced a profound alienation from the Church though most had overcome it, only to see it sometimes develop in their children. There was talk of extreme reluctance to contribute to the life of the Church ('fear' was the word used more than once). Was it similar experience that led to the assertion that if you speak out on matters of faith or on a current controversy in which church leaders have taken an interest, 'you get clobbered'?

'If you open your mouth to say what you think, if you speak independently, you can be made to feel outside the moral community.'

All those present agreed that, despite themselves, and by upbringing, tradition and education they were caught up in a 'negative theology'. They had not been taught how to love, but instead had been instructed how to avoid mistakes — by being totally obedient to Church authority. As one said, at the close of the day:

'This morning anything was possible. But look what happened. We have been tinkering around with the status quo. What would have *had* to happen to change us?'

Inevitably, as at any Christian gathering, there was for some the unspoken, unreasoning hope that the Spirit would be upon the meeting and all would be resolved, if only theoretically. Mostly, however, the contributions tempered frustration with acknowledgement that the Church was only two thousand years old and so had a long way to go.

There was no quarrel with the assertion that profitable dialogue between laity and hierarchy, and real enlightenment of church leaders would be impossible until those leaders recognised that dissidents were also church and honest conviction was acknowledged and welcomed. This sentiment came most often, and most forcefully phrased, from the elders of the meeting. The age of some dissidents might have been surprising, but even more interesting were the many speakers who revealed, despite themselves, the pervasiveness of the Irish Catholic tradition: of submission to authority; of the willingly informed conscience; of obedience to Rome. Even in this dedicated community at Bellinter, which grew in solidarity during the day, this conditioned, fiercely resented, but pervasive obedience to ecclesiastical authority could only be partly purged.

'We *expect* ourselves to be totally subservient'.

It seemed obvious that the conclusions of a synod on the laity would be less than persuasive if laity were not present and voting beside their bishops. It was feared that 'subservience' would again be expected of such few lay men and women as might be admitted, and that they would be unlikely to give the synod 'much useful information'.

Sisters and Brothers
From the likely composition of the synod it seemed to the meeting that the Church was curiously unaware of the signs of the times; that it had not appropriated the values of the twentieth century: the equality of men and women, of clergy and laity. The synod would suffer specially from the silence of women, who under the present regime were not allowed to speak to the Church from their own experience, and who were sometimes intimidated but more often repelled by massed lines of mitred male authority.

Women must not be afraid to ask: 'Why are we not up there?'

However the subject of womens' ordination was not a major topic during the long discussion. Perhaps this was because it became clear that there was a dense undergrowth of prejudice and misunderstanding to be cleared away (in matters sacred as well as in matters profane) before the subject could be seen in sane ecclesiastical or sociological perspective. Still, one woman said: 'Time we stopped writing and talking. We need to *do* it'.

The tone of all discussion was quiet; not angry. It was clear, just the same, that it was hard for women to feel they were fully part of a church where, as a matter of general policy, authority was given to those in holy orders, and holy orders were bestowed only on men. Through lack of understanding, (often because they were not married), some of these men had estranged women from the Church — women who could help to bring back compassion into the community, who had traditionally been supportive and who, especially in the family, have the gift of bonding individuals and making them one. This was a gift needed in the Church and in a world threatened by fragmentation. It was a gift often put to good use to preserve the dignity of an unemployed husband (it was a sign of the times that this observation was made more than once).

In many cases, the meeting felt, clerical understanding of the feminine was derived from devotion to an ethereal vision of the Blessed Virgin. This was said to be associated in some clerics with a marked reluctance to make friends with living women who, apart from anything else, might well help them to understand the full meaning of Mary's role. It was common ground among men and women present that, despite many saintly examples to the contrary — like Theresa and Catherine — masculine authority had tried to impose a strange ideal of feminine humility and of womanly self-sacrifice. However there were hopeful signs of a reversal of the old order in the World Council of Churches' dialogue about the community of women and men in the church:

'If we women feel oppressed by authority perhaps it is the same for men? We must establish common bonds. We have not supported each other'.

There was some complaint that 'even in the Christian community' it was sometimes seen as not quite respectable to have a large family, and there was no argument that 'the culture of the times' was often inimical to family life. However it was contended by a significant section of the meeting that there were voices from many pulpits using 'family values' as a cliche, recruiting religion to perpetuate social forms; urging wives to love their unemployed husbands, not so much to bolster their dignity, but to help prevent public protest against the status quo by keeping the men off the streets. It was forgotten that Christianity was meant to be subversive of the established order.

In an echo of the earlier fear of 'being clobbered' there was a plea from many women for 'freedom to tell the truth', specifically on contraception. This lack of freedom, so it was said, caused alienation even between husbands and wives. It could be questioned whether 'freedom' here meant 'courage' and how much either arose from a climate of repression.

Anyway (this was a minority voice, heard with interest) the family was "a very dubious structure". There were many different kinds of family: like a kibbutz, a single-parent family, a common-law family, a broken family. The Church gave too much lip-service to the spirituality of the 'ideal' family when the greatest needs of many families were really secular, like how to bring up their children on unemployment assistance.

A place for clergy . . .

It was discovered once again, during the day's discussion, how useful it could be to avoid preconceptions. It was found possible to make better biblical sense of one aspect of the day's business by turning the debate about clerical domination on its head. Did it really make sense to talk of lay men and women wanting to be included in a clerically dominated church? What we should be trying to do was to include the clergy in what is basically a lay church! Again, a glance around any Sunday congregation would show that it would be more sensible for men to ask to be included in a church made up predominently of women.

'The meaning of the incarnation is that God asked to be included in the human community, which was an alienated community. Then Jesus asked to be included in the even more alienated communities of his time. What we should be trying to arrange is that those who are somehow privileged in our time should seek a place with those who are less privileged.

'The incarnation and redemption are a summons to us to ask to be allowed into the company of the more excluded. That is where the Church basically lies.

'We need the structures and the institutions. They give a certain service but where the more deprived and the more excluded are, *there* is God at work. There is where the kingdom is coming. There is where we seek to be included'.

In these terms it made sense for the laity to come together as a distinct grouping within the Church and invite the clergy to join them, as the laity themselves should seek to join with those less privileged.

But the Bellinter consensus was that laity were apprehensive about approaching clergy. Many who had forged a place in the community for themselves did so in spite of the clerical power structure.

'The Vatican Council opened up the idea of lay participation in the life of the Church; but it is the clerical church which measures out the participation'.

There were some who contended that parish priests too had an argument: that they often called for volunteers and nobody came. They could claim that it was parishioners themselves who were at fault; that they were content to let things drift.

It was agreed that most people didn't want to get actively involved in church affairs just as they didn't want to get involved in politics. However this observation was countered with the assertion that everybody could gradually be involved in the life of the Christian community in an important way (as everybody is gradually involved in politics), if there was public debate within the community when important decisions were to be made. The people had received many gifts from the Church and from the world. Why were they not encouraged to share them?

Perhaps recent bishops' pastorals failed to connect because they had been written and promulgated without the advice of the people, much less their universal consent? What price Newman, not to speak of Vatican II!

The wish from all present at the meeting was that church leaders should begin to divest themselves of power so that they could achieve an authority born of service to the community. Then they would be seen to be truly a part of the Christian enterprise, and their pronouncements more readily heeded.

Generation Gap

Many of the people voicing criticisms confessed to being middle class — and uncomfortable about it. They had been lulled into a certain conformity with the status quo, or they saw themselves in imminent danger of this fate. However, at the same time, they wanted to help to build a just society. They were awaiting an authentic challenge.

'Our church allows us comfortable middle-class people to drift on saying a few prayers and not doing very much about the poverty and injustice around us'.

'The inextricable mixture, the poverty of the rich and the riches of the poor, is vital to our identity as church'.

Somebody sang:
'I come like a prisoner to bring you a key
The need of another is the gift that I bring
By the hungry I will feed you
By the poor I make you rich
By the broken I will mend you
Tell me, which one is which'

(Sidney Carter)

Those present knew very well that many of the people most concerned to spread the good news were not among them. They were about their Father's business elsewhere, convinced the Church was not listening to them. They had switched off from its one-way, top-down 'dialogue'. They included a signficant number of young people and other Christians working with the poor and the dispossessed. They did not relate at all to the institution or to the parish and did not wish to be identified as 'church people'. They might profess Gospel values, indeed they might live by them. But they could not share the hierarchical vision the Church had of itself. For these activists the real Church is people, and to think in terms of clergy and laity was implicitly to think of church as institution.

'Many people concerned with human rights and penal reform are not churchgoers'.

'People involved in social service do not wish to be identified as "church people"'.

'It is stultifying to be a churchgoing Catholic'.

It was said that there were now two typical reasons for 'leaving the church', two different ways of making an exit. Some young people who accepted the challenge of modern injustice were opting out of the sacramental life because they saw it as rigid and irrelevant. Others were dismayed by the uncertainties of modern life: from unemployment to the nuclear threat. They faced a crisis of faith and found no help in the insights of the post-Council years. So there was also a swing to the right (sometimes right out of the church), in the search for *certainty.*

More than one parent felt they should be able to help their sons and daughters from their own experience, but that experience had often put them at odds with authority.

'For many of us the religion we lived by was dismantled by Vatican II and we are left with only a few basic struc-

71

tures which our sons and daughters view with youthful honesty. They say what they see. Many of their concerns are silently shared by their parents. But the parents have grown to accept that they can't do anything about them'.

'We need to look outward. We seem too often to be trying to break back into the church. Instead we need to break out of structures. The people of God need to find new ways to know themselves'.

'Has the decline in a belief in hell made any difference? To what extent was obedience based on fear?'

Said one woman:
'In religion and society we are on the crest of a wave of change and we don't know where it is going to land us. We can't know what the future holds for our children. Already they are different from us in their spirituality, their life styles and as social beings'.

'Almost unconsciously and imperceptibly our children are living a life we don't understand. If we want to find our what the future holds we must observe them carefully'.

'There is a rule of prophesy: "We should listen to the wisest of the youth"'.

'The way things are is not the only way things can be but we are talking as if it was'.

Communion and Community

Even at the parish Mass on Sunday, the most fundamental action of the christian life, most saw a contrast between the idea of the People of God and the actual scene in the church. They said there was a lack of any real sense of community at Mass. There was the conventional regret about this. However, it was interesting that at no time during the discussion was there any radical criticism of liturgical practice.

Could this have been due to lack of experience of alternative ways of celebrating? Perhaps these fifty christians had been rather lucky in their parish experience?

There was the suggestion that perhaps the lack of community inside the parish church was inevitable since there was no community outside it. The gathering at the eucharist should be an affirmation and a celebration of a community already existing. Community groupings do exist but too often the attitude of the clergy, so it was said, was 'We didn't think them up, therefore we refuse to recognise them' whereas what all priests should do — as some do already — was discern the meaning of the Credit Union, even the GAA and the darts club *in terms of gospel.*

But there was one voice adding a specific complaint to the chorus of general lament for lack of community-in-liturgy. The complaint was this: The community is supposed to welcome a child at baptism and the ceremony is supposed to be during Mass on Sunday. Why, then, do most parish churches arrange most baptisms outside Mass when only the family is present? And then (with mounting conviction): 'What is the point of the church at all? What is the reason for the christian church?'

There was a subject proposed for debate some other time: Do you need more structures to tackle these omissions and to generate a proper sense of community? Or do you need fewer?

Somebody said:

'To set up a small community within the parish is to set up an alien structure. We can be stifled in small groups'.

Somebody else said:

'What you have to do is to unite minorities around primary goals'.

Given the top-down ecclesiastical structures now in place, the question was asked repeatedly: How can the laity get involved in defining goals in their own villages, cities and parishes? And how on earth can they get involved at world level in the Roman Synod?

A bishop had said to one of those present:

"I'll tell you how much the Irish bishops' submission will

rate in the final document. It will get one-and-a-half lines'.

Could the tension between local needs and desires and the many instructions from distant Rome be resolved if small groups of christians once again came together in table-fellowship to find Christ in one another, and so find his place in their own lives? Could they gain strength in this fellowship to move outward together in mission?

There was a ready acknowledgement that it might well be impossible to define a globally valid method of involving clergy and laity together in the life of the church, no matter how hard the synod tried in 1987. But at Bellinter it seemed to some that a start could be made if priests and people could jointly face real and present social issues; if together they could greet the poor and the young and the unemployed and unmarried mothers and fully accept them. But others observed that, ironically, while unmarried mothers were gradually being accepted, more and more of their married sisters felt themselves excluded.

'There is no sense of fellowship in the local church; no warmth; no relationship'.

Love and Law

For some speakers the reason many young marrieds who still believed in Christ felt outside the fellowship and stopped churchgoing was 'the near impossibility of "obeying and begetting" within the law'.

The church they know seems unaware of 'hierarchy of truths'; that there must be unity in essentials, freedom in non-essentials and charity in all things. Some said they did go to church, despite differences of opinion on aspects of sexual morality, 'but the complete impossiblity of putting your point of view to those in church authority is so hope-less . . .' The 'final incredibility' was that they were being asked to obey laws about sexual behaviour by people who had no personal experience in the matter.

Mothers and fathers present confessed they had no advice to offer their children. Again and again it seemed that the teaching of the Roman Catholic church did not coincide with what many of these christians believed; that it did not share their priorities; that they were concerned about justice while the church seemed more concerned about law.

And after all the talk about alienated women: 'Are there no alienated men?' – this from a totally female discussion group. And it seemed the men were not *so* alienated, but those in middle-age shared their wives' regret for a lack of tenderness in their religious upbringing.

A woman said:

'We were brought up not to know about love because we couldn't love ourselves. It was all about avoiding *traps'*.

Lack of tenderness and understanding from the teaching church had, for many people, accentuated the inevitable crisis of faith that came with emergence to adulthood. Those present had survived the crisis, but more than one of them questioned the need for so acute a crisis of faith. Nobody tried to define what 'acute' meant, but it was obvious that for many the experience had been painful but essentially irrelevant, and that it had arisen from the worship of a false 'God of the traps'.

All day the interventions carried undercurrents of both hope and foreboding. Thus: 'The children are leaving, but they are the ones who are going to survive on our behalf. We must focus on them." One of the most important missions, therefore, was to encourage the young to ministry; to service. Perhaps what was needed was a peer ministry, especially for youth? But in any case it would be a ministry shared jointly by clergy and laity 'a ministry that one is and does'. But for young children it seemed that the ministry of priest and parent could often be contradictory.

A woman wondered what to do when priests taught her children a religion of rules and regulations, while she wanted to tell them about love and fulfillment. 'Do I end up losing the friendship of my children in order to stand up for what I believe? What do I tell them?'

Ministry and Power

Irish history had given great moral power to the priesthood – and they were naturally slow to abandon it. However one group suggested that the best tactic was to get the trust of the clergy by finding out what they wanted to do and helping them to do it. After that they might be more inclined to return the favour by helping to achieve 'what you wanted to do yourselves'.

This group sympathised with the typical priest who had to reveal the gospel message to a large and diverse congregation. It also recognised that the power-structures posed problems for both priest and layman. The priest was in many cases subject to a bishop who could transfer him at short notice. To protect himself and others from the trauma of broken parish friendships, he might well give up trying to be a pastor and assume instead the role of distant lawgiver.

All in all, any resentment was not of 'priestly function' but of the structure in which it was imprisoned. It must be liberated to serve and bear witness.

The priesthood was to preside at the celebration of Mass, and to administer the sacraments, but apart from that wasn't ministry a collective function of clergy and laity? And was it not true that some lay men and women had a gift for some ministries that was denied their clergy?

There was a welcome for the introduction of 'ministers of the eucharist', particularly women ministers. But didn't the laity have a private as well as a public ministry, and in this context was there not a question about the practice of public commissioning of lay ministers? Was not ministry not only something you did but something you *were?* And didn't all these considerations point the need once again to redefine the laity's relationship with the clergy?

People couldn't make up their minds about church structures. They were prepared to accept the set-up until something better came along, but there were doubts whether it could show the world 'how these christians love one another'. The general opinion was that Vatican II said there should be a real effort to make the church into a community. But : . .

The hierarchical model was medieval with little contemporary relevance to reality. But it was the only model we have. There was a distant vision shared by all at Bellinter: a vision of a single community on pilgrimage to the kingdom: pope, bishops, priests and people all together. But there was a big gap between this vision and reality.

Meanwhile it was all right to hack away at structures while giving them provisional acceptance. It was an ambiguous attitude — like the implications of the structure themselves — but nobody was bothered by ambiguity. "Why are we always so anxious to arrive at a consensus about everything?'

'Why are we looking for certainty? Life is contingent. The only certainty is death'.

'Before the Council, we were all *Children* of God. Then we were promoted to being *People.* That was great because we all wanted to be adults in the faith, but all we have managed to do is to grow to be spiritual teenagers; defiant but insecure. We know that the priests and the bishops don't fully trust us to manage our relationships with each other or with God'.

'Why does the teaching church not trust its people? It should teach, certainly, but at some stage it should make a leap of faith and trust the Spirit working in the community'.

Whatever about the workings of the Spirit, the view from the floor of this meeting was that it was the cleric who had the power. Evidence was given: in one parish in Dublin's inner city useful structures grew simply because the parish priest enabled them. Laity ought to be able to generate parish structures but it was agreed that this would not happen until there was a shift of power. The people needed to come together and pool their talents to tackle the big parish problems. But was a parish a sensible unit in a big city and, if it was, need the priest who presided at the Eucharist be asked to preside at everything else?

There was a preoccupation with the nature and sources of power. One person said: 'I speak, therefore now I have power. Have I power because I am speaking or because this group has given me permission to speak? Where does power come from? How do we begin to take power?'

'Why can't we say: "The Gospel says do this" — so just do it and forget about the structures?'

'We need to reclaim our story. It's a question of discovering that our story and other peoples' story is one and the same at the heart of things. It's the Jesus story'.

As one listened to the discussion it was obvious that these christians were trying hard to reclaim the Jesus story and the two commandments at the heart of it: to love God and neighbour. They saw this as a personal and a communal responsibility and obviously thought the synod of bishops unreasonable to discuss it without taking them into their confidence. Their reference would have been to the Council's Dogmatic Constitution on the Church:

'. . . the Holy Spirit makes holy the People, leads them and enriches them with his virtues. Allotting his gifts according as he wills, he also distributes special graces among the faithful of every rank. By these gifts he makes them fit and ready to undertake the various tasks and offices for the renewal and building up of the church . . .'

It would be too much to say that the fifty men and women at Bellinter reached consensus. But in trying to see and speak the truth they did reach a unity of purpose which, at the end of the day, was resolved and expressed in a celebration of Word and Sacrament and a memorable sharing of ministry.

78

Afterword:
The Plain People of God

Seán MacRéamoinn

Sunday Mass in an Irish-speaking parish forty-odd years ago was little different from anywhere else in rural Ireland. The blessed mutter of the Latin, a silent congregation telling their beads; no visible or audible sign of a way of faith formed in and by the Gaelic tradition over fifteen hundred years.

But for one thing! As the priest turned to address those present, he did not greet them as his Dear Brethren. Instead, unbelievably, preserved from across the centuries:

> *. . . a phrase*
> *as, in wild earth, a Grecian vase.*

For his salutation was *A Phobail Dé:* People of God!

I cannot pretend that when I first heard the phrase at that Gaeltacht Mass forty odd years ago I was struck by its significance. Any more than were, I fancy, those around me, to whom it was a familiarly conventional greeting.

Today its familiarity is universal in the post-Conciliar Church, and familiarity has bred, if not contempt, a certain lack-lustre. Yet it was one of the great shining phrases of the Renewal, a talisman of liberation, of identity, of belonging: a confirmation that all of us − thinker, teacher, preacher, priest; bad man, sad man, sinner, saint − *all* of us, as we are and where we are, are absolutely and irrevocably His . . . *We* are the Church.

The implications of this basic truth are today only slowly, very slowly, coming to be realised: some of them indeed we can but guess at, and only the future will make them plain. If this is the case nearly twenty years after *Lumen Gentium,* it can be readily understood how a generation raised in the tradition of Church as Pyramid was at first intoxicated and then bewildered by the new vision.

Or, rather, an old vision which had been lost or mislaid and now was re-discovered. After all, even the most authoritarian of catechisms told us that the Church was 'the congregation of all the faithful', not just the pope-bishops-priests-nuns-brothers as we might have thought. However the latter was what we persisted in thinking, and as we thought we talked, and wrote.

> *He has two sons in the Church and another a doctor . . .*
> *He left all his money to the Church; the cousins didn't get*
> *a penny . . . The youngest went for the Church but he left*
> *and got married . . .*

That's the way *we* talked. But we weren't responsible for saying 'the Church teaches this', or 'the Church condemns that', or, at least, not primarily responsible. Some of those most assiduous in reminding us of our duties as *members* of the Church, the congregation of all the faithful, took a rather stricter line when identifying the Church as teacher, guide and ruler.

Whatever the Church had to say about the Immaculate Conception, or Anglican orders, or 'artificial' contraception, or General Franco, or education, or Communism, or 'immodest' dances was something said not *by* but *to* the faithful. Church meant church authority, and indeed, more often than not, authority personalised in Pope, or bishop. It was for them specifically or, more generally, for the magisterium to make, to *give* the ruling: and for the rest of us to receive. Such reception of the ruling given, acceptance without questioning, was in fact the very sign and proof of being one of the 'faithful'.

The division of the Church into givers and receivers held good in areas other than those of authority and discipline. Or perhaps we should say, that these were maintained throughout the Church's life by a dichotomy which was generally seen as God-given. And so they moulded and formed the expression of that life at its very core, in the ministries of Word and Sacrament.

Both these ministries were seen to involve custody as well as communication, and the first of these as a most serious and sacred trust necessitating disciplines of the strictest kind. Thus God's word in scripture, while meant for the nourishment of all, must not be lightly broadcast, rather should it be carefully and frugally dispensed in such a manner as might not disturb the immature understanding of simple people. Indeed the notion of the 'giving' Church as a kind of sacred *dispensary* is not too much of a distortion of how it was seen from the receiving end, especially in relation to the Sacraments. The graces of the Eucharist, Penance and Anointing were dispensed by the priest, as were those of Confirmation and Holy Orders by the bishop; Baptism was also effected by priests, except in an 'emergency', and Matrimony too was commonly regarded as being performed by a priest, despite constant reminders that the bride and groom were the real ministers of the Sacrament.

Still again the record demands mention of the not inconsiderable attempts to make the laity aware of 'their part' in the liturgy as a whole, going back to the time of St Pius X. For this Pope, in whose reign a deeply insensitive purge of 'modernists' took place, must be nevertheless honoured for his initiatives designed to encourage a less passive congregational attitude, especially to the Mass. On one level he encouraged popular involvement in the sung liturgy: this met with some limited success, although in Ireland, with a few shining exceptions, it didn't get much farther than the holding of one-day 'Liturgical Festivals' of school choirs. Far more fundamental was another papal initiative, permitting and indeed urging early and frequent reception of Holy Communion. Slowly but surely this became common, and already in Pius XII's time, certain concessions in relation to the eucharistic fast made for easier access.

Again though, as late as the Conciliar debate itself, a restrictive view of the place of the Bible in lay spirituality lingered on, Catholics were encouraged to read the New Testament especially (though, for a long time, in 'properly' annotated editions), privately and in study groups. And at Sunday Mass, the epistle and/or gospel was often repeated in the vernacular, after the liturgical reading in Latin: however, a restricted cycle of readings was a serious obstacle to any broad biblical pedagogy. And, of course, lay involvement in the actual proclamation of the Word in the assembly was unthinkable — almost as unthinkable as that a lay man or woman should distribute Holy Communion!

Still the 'dispensary' model prevailed in practice and, on the whole, in theory — although there were new ideas abroad, or rather a rediscovery of old ideas and old ways. With the single very important exception of frequent general communion, the Church at Mass at the turn of the half-century was as it had been for many hundreds of years, going back far beyond Trent in a practice rooted in early medieval abuses, clericalist in ideology and exclusivist in effect, which built a wall between the clergy and the plain people of God.

If, as I have suggested, the very words 'People of God' have lost something of their splendour, this has not been altogether due to over-repetition but because we are still divided into givers and receivers, active members and passive. Not indeed as strictly as before: for not alone have the laity entered the sanctuary, and lawfully laid hands on the mysteries; not alone in the office of reader, and — all but in name — the diaconate, practised by wives and daughters as well as by their men-folk; not alone is the congregation no longer silent — but all this is in some way reflected, to some extent interiorised, in the way we, the faithful, think of ourselves and our role.

But the reflection, the interiorisation are only partial, and, I believe, mainly confined to the domain of worship. Our more active role in the liturgy may well make us realise that we are part of the worshipping Church: but I doubt if we carry any similar realisation into our everyday lives. I mean, when the word 'church' comes into our conversation when we read it or hear it on the radio, do we think of *our* membership, *our* role? Or if we do, do we think of those as active or merely passive?

I am not here bringing faith or fidelity into question. On the contrary, devotion and docility are often found among the most passive and indeed among those who still regard 'the Church' as *other*: an institution, benevolent, even essential to their well-being in this world and the next, to be regarded and listened to with respect, loyalty, obedience. To these the Church is still the Church of pulpit, altar, confessional: more specifically the clergy.

If it is true, as I have suggested, that many, perhaps most, of the devout still think this way, it is certainly also true of the *un*-devout, of those who (whether inside or outside) regard the Church with hostility, cynicism, derision — or pretend to do so. If they include the laity in their criticisms or strictures, it is as accessories, dupes, lackeys, not as the real villians — that role is reserved for the clergy. And, by and large, I think it would be fair to say that more objective commentators and students of the eccesiastical scene — sociologists and the like — would tend to a similar distinction.

Now the clergy themselves, on all levels, are by no means free from responsibility for the maintenance of what should be seen as an imperfect and an anachronistic view of the Church. In terminology as well as in attitude, they far too often support the giver/receiver, active/passive division, although in all fairness many, perhaps most, would not consciously wish to do so. Unfortunately, good intentions are never enough: one recalls the story of the kindly prelate stressing the equality before God of all his people, 'from the bishop down'!

If, then, the plain People of God are not alone in lack of full appreciation of their status and vocation, is this just another example of less than assiduous, less than enthusiastic, communication of the teaching of Vatican II? Or is it possible that there may be something lacking in that teaching, that the Conciliar vision which lit and transformed so much of our spiritual landscape faltered somewhat in this, as in some other areas?

The role of the laity is discussed in the Constitutions on the Liturgy and the Church in the Modern World (Gaudium et Spes), as in the Decrees on the Lay Apostolate, Ecumenism and, indeed, Social Communication. But the basic document is the Constitution on the Church, *Lumen Gentium.*

This has well been called the *Magna Carta* of the laity, though it would be unfortunate if historical extrapolation led to any suggestion of rights hard-won from an unwilling tyrant! On the contrary, the whole Constitution, in form as in content, brings a new perspective to bear on the issue, in placing its consideration of the People of God immediately after its initial exposition of the Mystery of the Church, and before any discussion of hierarchical structure.

Truly this second chapter of the Constitution proclaiming, in Peter's words, 'a chosen race, a royal priesthood, a holy nation . . . who in times past were not a people, but now are the People of God', should be made regular required re-reading for us all. Lest we forget. For with splendid balance, and in language as free from text-book aridity as from pious pseudo-lyricism, it describes the messianic people, their common priesthood to the world, their Catholic witness, their mission. In a word it recalls us to our vocation.

This is spelt out further, and even more clearly, in chapter five of the Constitution: 'The call to Holiness'. Here the universal force of Christ's words 'You, therefore, must be perfect as your heavenly Father is perfect' is seen to bind on all his disciples without distinction: 'the forms and tasks of life are many but holiness is one'. However, the chapter points at the same time to the modes of response to Christ's call adhering to these 'several forms and tasks'.

Between these two chapters on the People of God and the Call to Holiness there are two others: 'The Church is Hierarchical' and 'The Laity'. The first of these deals with the ordained ministry or ministries — bishops, priests, deacons. The great strength of this chapter is, of course, the way in which it identifies and clarifies the role of the episcopate, individually and collectively, thus redressing an apparent imbalance in relation to the Papal Primacy, due to the 'unfinished business' of Vatican I.

The implications of this new emphasis were widely hailed at the time of the document's promulgation, on two counts. On the one hand it seemed to underline the autonomy of the local church by pointing to the role of the bishops 'as vicars and legates of Christ (who) govern the particular Churches assigned to them . . . The pastoral charge . . . is entrusted to them fully; nor are they to be regarded as vicars of the Roman Pontiff.'

To complement this, the rediscovery of collegiality, would, it was confidently believed, enrich the Church catholic; the bishops, joined together with the Pope at their head, would, in a great confederation of local traditions and charisms, preside over a new and resplendent unity, unencumbered by the rigidities of uniformity. I think it reasonable to say that this vision has so far been only very partially realised.

It would be beyond my present brief to speculate to what extent bureaucratic centralism has frustrated the full exercise of episcopal collegiality. What I would wish to note is that almost from the beginning it became clear that the collegial idea itself was not likely to extend *beyond* the college of bishops to any significant degree. The hope that it would be reproduced in the local church i.e. the bishop as head of a presbyteral government — and thence in the parish, with the pastor presiding over a lay council — was never really on. That is not to say that experiments in devolutionary democracy of a consultative kind have not taken place, but, apart from a few brief essays of a more radical nature, diocesan and parochial government remains in the pattern of monarchy, though admittedly of a more constitutional brand than heretofore.

It may be going too far to say that the kind of imbalance which over-emphasised the role of the Papacy in Vatican I is matched in relation to the episcopate in Vatican II. But compared to the rich and subtle treatment of the bishop's office, *Lumen Gentium* is comparatively weak on the ministerial priesthood. It is however in regard to the Laity that one detects an unsureness of touch which I believe has contributed to continuing ambiguities as to who are the Church.

The second paragraph of the laity chapter reads:

> The term 'laity' is here understood to mean all the faithful except those in Holy Orders and those who belong in a religious state approved by the Church. That is, the faithful who by Baptism are incorporated into Christ, are placed in the People of God, and in their own way share the priestly, prophetic and kingly office of Christ, and to the best of their ability carry on the mission of the whole Christian people in the Church and in the world.

One might suspect that phrases like 'in their own way' and 'to the best of their ability' show a certain patronising attitude to those neither in Holy Orders nor in 'a religious state'. But I think this would be wrong: the chapter as a whole is generous in its appreciation of those who try to live the Gospel in a fully secular life. It does honour to marriage and the family, to work for political and social justice, and to all those activities which go to build up the Body and constitute 'a sharing in the salvific mission of the Church'. Furthermore, while the laity are urged to 'collaborate with their pastors and teachers', so also should the pastors 'recognise and promote the dignity and responsibility of the laity . . use their prudent service . . . leaving them freedom and scope for acting . . . consider attentively in Christ initial moves, suggestions and desires proposed by the laity . . . and respect and recognise the liberty which belongs to all in the terrestrial city'.

We have come a long way from such definitions of the role of the laity as 'to beget and to obey'! Rather in its emphasis on fraternal solidarity between pastors and people it returns to the spirit and words of St Augustine:

When I am frightened by what I am to you then I am consoled by what I am with you. To you I am the bishop, with you I am a Christian. The first is an office, the second a grace; the first a danger, the second salvation.

No uncertainty there. But it would be idle to pretend that something has not been lost since Augustine's time and not fully recovered in our own. Or, to put it another way, something has crept in, intruded into the fold, that we might well now be rid of. In a word, I mean *clericalism,* and particularly the confusion between cleric and minister.

The definition of 'laity' in *Lumen Gentium,* quoted above has one basic flaw: it is negative. While describing the vast majority of the Baptised, it seems to see them as a 'remnant', all the faithful *minus* the ordained and the 'religious'.

There is nothing new in this kind of definition. My dictionary explains the adjective *lay* as 'pertaining to the people; not clerical; non-professional' . . . *laity* as 'the people as distinguished from some particular profession, usu. the clerical'. But of course we are all accustomed to the usage in relation to law, medicine and so on. So it is not unfair to say that, Church affairs apart, 'lay' and 'laity' tend to imply non-professional, uninformed, amateur. But not in Church affairs? I wonder. Can we really draw the line we might like to feel exists?

To call the priesthood a profession may shock pious ears: but substitute the word 'clergy' and it's not so bad. Certainly, few would deny the clergy their place among the *learned* professions. Indeed in the past they have on occasion found allies and (almost) equals in these *metiers.* It has in fact been remarked that some allegations of clerical arrogance or authoritarianism could have been with equal justice made in relation to lawyers and doctors, not least in their shared reluctance to admit the existence of, let alone listen to, an informed *laity.* It was in this sort of context, among others, that the *Church* was seen as the clergy, the clergy as profession — and indeed a professional class of considerable power and prestige. 'Church' in this sense was no more seen to include the laity than patients in the county hospital were medical practitioners.

This is not the place to rehearse the lengthy process by which the ministers of the Christian Church became the clerks and administrators of Euope. Nor need we question the province of God who allowed the preaching of the Gospel to become so involved with the processes of secular civilisation that medieval history was forced to repeat itself in joining the Church's outreach with that of secular Europe in modern times. At least recent experience can show how a good custom can corrupt and be corrupted.

We do not have to beat our breasts for the sins, let alone the misjudgements, of our fathers nor with Olympian hindsight, condemn the Constantinian settlement and all that followed· from it as A Bad Thing. But neither does the historical explanation of an abuse justify its continuance. The Council was exemplary in the way in which it grasped a number of nettles which had too long been regarded as sacred flora. But the clerical weed continues to grow thick and fast, or at least, shows no sign of withering.

I have no doubt that this is so, mainly because we do not yet recognise it as a weed, and a noxious one at that. Or, to vary the metaphor, a poison in the Body. That it is ubquitous, endemic, in the Church — at least in the West — few would deny. But its close association with ministry has led it to being regarded as beneficial, even necessary. At times it seems that it is actually equated with ministry itself: that cleric and minister have the same meaning.

I have searched the Conciliar documents for a definition of 'clergy' which I might justapose with that of 'laity': the best I have been able to come up with is the following, not from any of the Constitutions or Decrees, but from the *postconciliar* 'Apostolic Letter on First Tonsure, Minor Orders and the Subdiaconate':

It is more in keeping with the nature of the case and with

contemporary attitudes that such ministries should no longer be called 'minor orders' . . . *Only those who have received the diaconate will be, and will be called, clerics* (my italics).

In so far as that rationalises a previously illogical and anachronistic situation, well and good. The reduction of the offices of minor orders to two, reader and acolyte, was sensible, and their exercise by lay people widely welcomed. (The Apostolic Letter, incidentally, reserves them to men only 'in keeping with the venerable tradition of the Church.')

But the implied identification of 'clerics' with those who have received (at least) the diaconate is interesting and, I believe, unfortunate. For taking this along with the constitutional definition of the laity, we would now appear to have three categories in the People of God: clergy; religious (some of whom may also be clergy) and the rest. May I repeat: what I find unacceptable in this is the *negative* character given to the overwhelming lay majority, what defines them is that they are neither clergy nor members of a community of 'religious' (and that word begs a few questions too!).

As is made clear over and over again in this volume not alone history and etymology but sound theology would rather suggest that the laity, the *Laos,* is in fact the whole People of God, *from among whom* some are called to the three-fold ministry of Orders, some to the dedication and commitment of a religious rule, but in neither case losing their lay status, which is in fact their membership of Christ's body, sacramentally engaged at Baptism. The priesthood of the laity is no more fundamental than the 'layhood' of the priest (or nun, or bishop).

It should not be necessary to say (but probably is) that I neither intend nor desire any derogation of either the ministry or the 'religious' life. Nor do I wish to see any blurring of the special position of the ministry of Orders, among the many offices and charisms in the Church. On the contrary I am convinced that declericalisation would immensely strengthen the ministerial office and identify it more clearly as an indispensable service to and within God's people.

I am well aware that this would involve a complex, subtle and at times painful process, a stripping of the very integument within which the ministry has so long lived, moved and had its being. To many, inside as well as outside, it would appear as if the very fabric of the Church itself was being systematically demolished. Nor do I pretend that the process could or should be lightly undertaken, or without careful preparation and research — as well as the most sensitive concern for individual hardships, spiritual and material, consequent on the removal of familiar structures and supports. For after all what we have in mind is the destruction of a *class* and the freeing of a vocation.

It is not chiefly or even significantly a question of privilege. Phrases like 'reduction to the lay state' (laicisation) may rankle, but the offence to theology is more important than that to the *cosmhuintir*. Discrimination within the eucharistic assembly has all but disappeared: Communion under both kinds is conceded in principle, if only marginally in practice. In the larger arena 'clerical dress' (when worn) hardly secures many advantages, while in the higher reaches, titles like 'my lord' and the kissing of rings have almost disappeared.

My basic argument is threefold. Firstly that in a Church without a clerical class, a whole host of tasks and concerns, only remotely (if at all) connected with the ministry of Orders, would fall from the shoulders of priests and bishops, freeing them to see and act in a more directly pastoral way. Secondly, such of the responsibilities thus shed as authentically pertained to the Church's mission could be taken up by those among the unordained best qualified to assume them. And thirdly, serious questions about the ministry itself, such as celibacy and the ordination of women, could be looked at in a new perspective.

This then is a plea for the plain and unordained People of God. A plea that those gifts and talents of which the apostle speaks, those skills and specialisations acquired in learning to live their daily lives, be recognised and engaged in true ministries, supportive of those practised by our ordained brethren, and partaking in a new collegiality.

A plea for a renewal of the laos.

Appendix
Decree on the Apostolate of Lay People
A Summary

Austin Flannery OP

Introduction

1. Lay people have always had a special and indispensable role in the Church's ministry and the need for their contribution is even greater today. There are several reasons for this. The population of the world is increasing and at the same time travel and communications are easier. New problems have come to light which need the attention of lay people and many sectors of human life have become autonomous. Lastly, priests are scarce in many places and in some places obstacles are put in the way of their ministry.

The existence of the need is attested by the action of the Holy Spirit in making many lay people more deeply aware of their responsibility and impelling them to serve Christ and the Church.

This Decree will explain the nature of the lay apostolate and its many forms. It will state fundamental principles and will give pastoral directives for its more effective exercise.

Chapter 1
The vocation of lay people to the apostolate

Sharing in the Church's mission

2. The Church was founded, for the glory of God, to spread the kingdom of Christ and to redeem and save mankind, thus establishing a right relationship between Christ and the world. All activities with this end in view are called "apostolic" and they involve all the members of the Church in various ways. For the Christian vocation is of its nature a call to the apostolate and in the living Body of Christ purely

passive members are useless to the Church and to themselves.

There are many ministries in the Church, but one mission. Lay people have their part to play in teaching, sanctifying and governing in the Church and in the world, tasks entrusted in the first place to the apostles and to their successors. Lay people perform these tasks when they evangelise and sanctify men and women and also when they endeavour to permeate and improve the temporal order with the spirit of the gospel, witnessing to Christ and helping to save humankind. It is for them to be a leaven in the world in which they live.

Foundations of the lay apostolate

3. It is because they are united to Christ the head of the Church that lay people have the right and duty to be apostles and it is the Lord himself who appoints them through baptism and confirmation. A kingly priesthood and a holy nation, their activities are offered as a spiritual sacrifice and are a witness to Christ. At the heart of their ministry is charity, given to them and nourished by the sacraments, especially the eucharist.

Faith, hope and love, given by the Holy Spirit, are the life-blood of the apostolate. Love impels all Christians to work for the coming of God's kingdom and so that all may know him in eternal life. All Christians, accordingly, are obliged to carry God's message of salvation world-wide to all men and women.

The people of God are sanctified by the Holy Spirit through the ministry of the word and sacraments. Lay people are given special gifts also, however, which carry with them the right and the duty to use them in the Church and in the world for people's good and for the building-up of the Church. This they are entitled to do in the freedom of the Holy Spirit, but in collaboration with their brothers and sisters in Christ and especially with their pastors. For it is for pastors to judge whether the gifts are authentic and are being put to good use, but it is certainly not for them to quench the Spirit.

4. The apostolate of lay people will be fruitful if they live in union with Christ, the source of the apostolate, who said "separated from me you can do nothing" (John 15:5). There are spiritual helps, especially participation in the liturgy, for maintaining this union. There should be no separation, however, between people's union with Christ and their ordinary lives. Rather should their work be used to improve their union with him. Neither family cares nor any other temporal interest should be foreign to the spirituality of lay people. It is a life which calls for a life of constant faith, hope and love.

Only faith and meditation on the word of God enable us to find God everywhere and always, to seek his will in everything, to see Christ in all men and women and to judge the true meaning and value of temporal realities in themselves and in their bearing on life's purpose.

People with such a faith live in the hope of the revelation of the sons and daughters of God, mindful of the Lord's cross and resurrection. Their lives are hidden with Christ in God, they are freed from enslavement to riches and seek rather what will last for ever. They do their best to extend God's kingdom, to make the Christian spirit a vital, energising force in the temporal sphere, encouraged by their hope of future glory.

Prompted by God's love, they do good to all, especially their fellow Christians, eschewing "ill-will and deceit, all hypocrisy, envy and slander" (1 Peter 2:1). They try to give concrete expression to the Beatitudes in their lives. After the example of the poverty of Christ they do not find want depressing, nor plenty a source of pride, nor are they given to ostentation. They try to please God rather than men and women, are prepared to abandon all things for Christ and to endure persecution in the cause of right. They are friendly and supportive of one another.

The character of lay spirituality will vary according to whether a person is married, single or widowed and will vary with a person's state of health, job and social activity. Each person has been given talents and gifts of the Holy Spirit and should cultivate them.

Lay people who, in keeping with their calling, have joined a spiritual association or institution approved by the Church should try to make their own that body's form of spirituality.

They should hold in high esteem professional competence, a sense of family and civic sense, and also the virtues which mould behaviour in society: honesty, justice, sincerity, courtesy and moral courage. Without these there can be no true Christian life.

The Blessed Virgin is a perfect model for this apostolic spiritual life, devoted as she was to her work in the home and yet intimately united with her Son and collaborating with him in an entirely unique way in his saving work. All should be genuinely devoted to her. They should entrust their lives to her motherly care, now that, assumed into heaven, "her motherly love keeps her attentive to her Son's brothers and sisters."

Chapter II

Objectives

5. It was to redeem and save men and women, essentially, that Christ came on earth. However, the scope of his redemption takes in the temporal order too. The Church's mission, consequently, is not only to bring the message and grace of Christ to men and women, but also to permeate and improve this world. Lay people carry out their apostolate in the world as well as in the Church, in the temporal order as well as in the spiritual. It is God's plan to make of the world a new creation, to a limited extent here and now and fully at the end of time. Lay people, as citizens of the world and believers, have but a single Christian conscience, however, by which they must be guided in both domains.

Evangelisation and sanctification

6. The main task of the Church and of its members is to proclaim to the world by word and action the message of Christ, which activity is the ministry of the word, and to impart to the world the grace of Christ, the latter activity being the ministry of the sacraments. While the ministries are especially the task of the clergy, there is scope for lay people here too, complementing the work of the clergy.

Lay people can proclaim the word and sanctify people in countless ways. A good Christian life and good works can draw people to belief and to God. As the Lord said: "Your light must shine before men that they may see your good works and glorify your Father who is in heaven" (Matt 5:16). Further, they will seek opportunties of proclaiming Christ to unbelievers in order to draw them to belief, or to believers in order to instruct and strengthen them and to increase their fervour.

New questions are being asked nowadays and serious errors threaten to undermine religion, the moral order and human society itself. For this reason the Council urges lay people to take a more active part, in keeping with their abilities and in fidelity to the mind of the Church, in defending and explaining Christian principles and their correct application to the problems of our time.

The renewal of the temporal order

7. It is God's plan that men and women should renew the temporal order and perfect it. The temporal order is made up of family values, culture, economic matters, the trades and professions, political institutions, international relations and so on, as these develop. All of them are of value in themselves, individually and as parts of the entire. They are not just helps to people's last end, although their dignity is enhanced by their having been created for the use of men and women. It is further enhanced by virtue of the fact that it is God's purpose to gather together in Christ all that is natural and all that is supernatural. Nor does this deprive the tempor-

al order of its autonomy, its purpose, its laws and resources. Rather does it raise it here below to the level of the human vocation.

The use made of temporal things has at times been seriously defective. Because of original sin, people have erred about God, human nature and morality. This led to the corruption of human conduct and institutions and to even the human person being held in contempt. In our own time, an immoderate reliance on science and technology have led to a kind of idolatry of the temporal and enslavement to it.

It is the Church's task to form men and women able properly to evaluate the temporal order and direct it to God through Christ. Pastors should teach the purpose of creation and the use to be made of the world and should provide moral and spiritual helps for the renewal of the temporal order in Christ.

Lay people should take on the renewal of the temporal order as their distinctive task, guided by the Gospel and the Church and prompted by Christian love. They should bring their own special competence to their collaboration with their fellow citizens, acting on their own responsibility, always seeking the justice of the kingdom of God. Renewal should respect the nature of the temporal order, in harmony with the principles of the Christian life and in tune with the time, the location and the people. Social action is of the greatest importance here, extended to every sector of life, including the cultural sphere.

Charitable works and social aid
8. There are certain activities which are a most eloquent expression of that charity which should motivate the entire apostolate. Christ has willed that these should be the sign of his messianic mission (see Matt. 11:4-5).

Christ made the love of one's neighbour his own personal commandment and gave it new meaning when he included himself at the side of those to be loved: "When you showed it to one of the least of my brothers here, you showed it to me" (Matt. 25:40). When he became man he formed one human family in supernatural solidarity, making himself part of it. He made love the distinguishing mark of his followers: "By this will all men know you for my disciples, by the love you bear one another" (John 13:35).

In its early days the Church linked the "love-feast, the agape" to the eucharistic supper, thus revealing itself as one body grouped around Christ, united by love. Love is the Church's characteristic mark in all ages and it claims charitable works as its own mission and right, while rejoicing in their existence elsewhere. Consequently, the care of the poor and of the sick, works of charity and in alleviation of all kinds of human need are held in special honour in the Church.

The need for such activities is much more widespread and more urgent today, as easy communication and rapid travel have made of all mankind one family. Charitable activity can and should reach all people and all needs today. Wherever there are people in want of food and drink, clothing, housing, medicine, work, education, the means necessary for leading a truly human life, wherever there are people racked by misfortune or illness, suffering exile or imprisonment, Christian charity should seek them out, comfort and care for them devotedly and give them the help their needs require. This obligation falls in the first place on the richer individuals and nations.

If this charity is to be above criticism, the image of God must be perceived in one's neighbour and the image of Christ the Lord to whom is given what is given to the needy. The person's liberty and dignity must be respected with the greatest sensitivity. There must be no self-seeking or desire to dominate. Justice should be done first of all and what is due in justice must not be given as charity. The cause of evils must be removed and aid should be so organised that its beneficiaries gradually become self-supporting.

Lay people should therefore highly esteem and support as best they can private or public works of charity and social assistance movements, including international schemes. Effective help can thus be conveyed to individuals and nations in need, in collaboration with all men and women of good will.

Chapter III

Various apostolates

9. Chief among the apostolates open to the laity in the Church and in the world are: Church communities, the family, the young, the social environment, national and international spheres. It is important that the participation of women in the apostolate should develop, as it is developing in the rest of society.

Church communities

10. The involvement of lay people in the Church communities is so necessary that without it the apostolate of the pastors will not be fully effective. Apostolically minded lay people meets the needs of their fellow men and women and are a source of consolation to both pastors and community. Drawing nourishment from the liturgy, they engage in apostolic work, draw people towards the Church who may have been far away from it and help spread the word of God, especially by catechetical instruction. They make more effective both the care of souls and the administration of the property of the Church.

The parish is the outstanding example of community apostolate, granted the diversity of people which it inserts into the universal Church. Lay people should develop the habit of working in the parish in close union with their priests and of bringing before the ecclesial community their own problems, world problems and questions pertaining to men's and women's salvation, examining them together and solving them through discussion. Lay people ought to co-operate in all the apostolic and missionary enterprises of the ecclesial family according to their ability.

Lay people should cultivate a sense of the diocese of which the parish is a cell and should be ready to contribute to diocesan undertakings at the invitation of the bishop. Indeed, they should not limit their cooperation to the parish or diocese but should be prepared to extend it to interparochial, interdiocesan, national and international spheres. This is all the more necessary in view of present population shifts: no one part of society can live in isolation and lay people should extend their concern world-wide. They should be willing to give material and even personal help to the foreign missions.

The family
11. God made the married state the beginning and foundation of human society and, by his grace, a great mystery in Christ and in the Church. The apostolate of married people has thus a special importance for Church and society.

Christian couples are co-workers in the realm of grace and witnesses to the faith both in regard to each other, to their children and to their relatives. They are the first to pass on the faith to their children and to educate them in it, forming them to a Christian and apostolic life, guiding them in their choice of vocation and encouraging them if they find that they are called to the priesthood or the religious life.

It has always been the duty of married couples to provide proof of the indissolubility and holiness of marriage in their own lives, to assert the right and duty of parents and guardians to give their children a Christian upbringing and to defend the dignity and legitimate autonomy of the family. This duty is today the most important aspect of their apostolate. They should collaborate in safeguarding these rights in civil legislation and in ensuring that the requirements of families are met in housing, education and children, working conditions, social security and taxes and in regulations concerning emigration.

God gave the family the mission of being the primary cell of society, a mission which it will accomplish if by mutual affection and family prayer it behaves as a domestic sanctuary of the Church, takes part in the Church's liturgical worship, is hospitable and behaves justly and charitably towards those in want. The following are examples of a family apostolate: adopting abandoned children, welcoming strangers, helping to run schools, advising and helping adolescents, helping engaged couples to prepare for marriage, teaching catechism, supporting families in material or moral crises, providing for the elderly and ensuring that they share the fruits of economic progress.

Christian families witness to Christ when they remain attached to the gospel and offer an example of Christian marriage. This has everywhere and always been true, but it is especially the case where the Church has been recently established or is in crisis.

It can be apostolically advantageous if Christian families organise themselves in groups.

Young people
12. Young people have great importance in modern society. Their life-styles, ways of thinking and their relations with their famillies have been completely changed. Often they enter too rapidly a new social and economic environment. Their social and political importance is increasing, but they seem unequal to their new responsibilities.

Granted their increased social importance, they ought to be more involved in apostolic activity and indeed this is their natural inclination. Their energy and enthusiasm enables them to take on responsibilities as they mature and to take their place in social and cultural life. If this enthusiasm is penetrated with the spirit of Christ and animated with a sense of obedience and love for the pastors of the Church, a rich harvest can be expected. The young should be the first apostles of the young, contacting them directly, engaging in the apostolate themselves in their own social environment.

Adults should be prepared to dialogue with the young, getting to know them and to share with them. It is by their example especially, and also by advice and help, that they should persuade the young to undertake the apostolate. Young people will treat their elders with respect and confidence and, while predisposed towards what is new, will respect tradition.

Children too have an apostolate of their own, being witnesses to Christ in their own way among their companions.

Apostolate of like towards like
13. Exercising the apostolate in one's social environment means infusing the Christian spirit into the mentality, behaviour, laws and structures of the community. This is something that only lay people can do really well, conducting the apostolate of like towards like, the witness of their lives being completed by the witness of their word. They can best do this at work or leisure and where they live.

Lay people exercise their apostolate by that blend of behaviour and faith which makes them the light of the world; by being upright in their dealings, thus leading people to what is good and true and ultimately to Christ and the Church; by that charity which bids them share the living conditions, the work, the sufferings and the yearnings of their brothers and sisters, imperceptibly preparing all hearts for the action of saving grace; by full awareness of their responsibility for the development of society, leading them to be generous in doing their family, social and professional duties. In this way, their behaviour makes itself gradually felt where they live and work.

This apostolate should be aimed at every individual and should not exclude any possible spiritual or temporal good. Genuine apostles, however, will be anxious to speak of Christ to those about them. Many people have no hope of hearing the gospel unless they hear it from the lay people they encounter.

National and international levels
14. There is vast scope for the apostolate at national and international levels and it is here, especially, that lay people

are channels of Christian wisdom. Catholics who are patriotic and imbued with a sense of civic duty will want to promote the common good, the just exercise of civil authority and laws which accord with morality and the common good. Catholics who are politically able and firm in their faith and the Christian teaching should not decline to enter public life, where they can work for the common good and at the same time prepare the way for the gospel.

Catholics should gladly collaborate with people of good will in the promotion of what is true, holy and lovable, dialoguing with them, approaching them with understanding and courtesy, seeking ways of improving social and public institutions along the lines of the gospel.

A noteworthy sign of the times is the growing sense of solidarity among peoples. Lay apostles should develop this sense and transform it into a sincere desire for fraternal union. Lay people should be aware of the international sector and of the theoretical and practical problems and solutions emerging there, especially among under-developed nations.

People working abroad or helping foreign nations should remember that relations among peoples should be a real fraternal interchange of give and take. Travellers abroad should remember that they are messengers of Christ and should behave accordingly.

Chapter IV
Different forms of the apostolate

15. Lay people can exercise their apostolate singly or in groups.

Individual apostolate
16. The individual apostolate is the starting point of all apostolic activity; nothing can replace it. There is always scope for it and sometimes it is the only kind possible. Every lay person is called and indeed obliged to it, even if he or she has no opportunity for involvement in associations.

The lay apostolate can take many forms. A special form of individual apostolate is the witness of an entire life issuing from faith, hope and charity. It is a sign very much in keeping with our times, a manifestation of Christ living in his faithful. By the apostolate of the word, which is sometimes absolutely necessary, lay people proclaim Christ, explain and spread his teaching and are faithful to it.

Moreover, in all that pertains to the construction and development of the temporal order lay people should be guided and be seen to be guided by higher motives, in the light of faith, in the home, at work and in cultural and social life. They thus cooperate with God the creator, redeemer and sanctifier and give him glory.

Lay people should be charitable and as far as possible should practise works of charity. They should remember that they can reach all people and can contribute to the salvation of the world by public worship, prayer, penance and by willing acceptance of the toil and hardship of life after the manner of the suffering Christ.

Individual apostolate in certain circumstances
17. The individual apostolate is very much needed where the Church's freedom is severely limited. Where this happens, lay people take over the work of priests, endangering their freedom and sometimes their lives, teaching Christian doctrine, instilling a religious way of life, Catholic attitudes, the frequent reception of the sacraments and the cultivation of piety, especially eucharistic piety. The Council thanks God for the heroic courage of such lay people in the midst of persecution and it embraces them with gratitude and fatherly affection.

Where Catholics are few and scattered, the individual apostolate is particularly important and those who, for whatever reason, practise it can come together in small, informal groups for discussion. This ensures the continuing visibility of a sign of the Church as community, as witness to love. The experience of friendship and the exchange of experiences encourage such people to overcome the difficulties of too isolated a life, thus increasing the effectiveness of their apostolate.

Group apostolate
18. While the faithful are called to individual apostolates of various kinds, they should remember that men and women are social by nature and that God has willed to assemble believers in Christ into a single body, the People of God. The group apostolate is in accord with a fundamental need which is both human and Christian. It is a sign of the communion and unity of the Church in Christ who said: "Where two or three are gathered together in my name, I am there in the midst of them." (Matt 18:20).

Christians will exercise their apostolate in a spirit of concord in their families, their parishes, their dioceses, all of which already express the communal character of the apostolate, and in whatever free associations they will have formed.

The group apostolate is important when there is need for concerned action and also in the support it affords the members of the group and the training and direction it can give them; it is much more effective than if each were acting on his or her own.

There is great need nowadays for the strengthening of the collective lay apostolate if all the aims of the modern apostolate are to be achieved. People engaged in the apostolate should be au fait with the group attitudes and social conditions of those who are the object of their attentions, who otherwise may be unable to withstand the pressure of public opinion or of social institutions.

Various kinds of group apostolate
19. There is a great variety of apostolic associations, some with the Church's over-all apostolate in view, others specialising in evangelisation and sanctification, others endeavouring to permeate the temporal order with the Christian spirit and

still others witnessing to Christ by works of mercy and charity.

First among the associations to be considered are those which attempt to bring their members' everyday lives into conformity with their belief. Associations are not ends in themselves; they are meant to serve the Church's mission to the world. Their apostolic value will be in proportion to their conformity with the Church's aims and to their apostolic spirit and that of their members.

The Church's universal mission requires that by their apostolic initiatives Catholics should make international organisations more perfect, granted their development and the rapid evolution of modern society. International Catholic organisations will be more successful the greater the cohesion between them and the groups and members which comprise them.

Granted the requisite link with ecclesiastical authority, lay people have the right to establish and manage organisations and to join existing ones. They should avoid spreading themselves too thinly, however. This can happen when, without sufficient justification, new organisations are formed and new enterprises started. It can also happen through failure to have done with obsolete methods and with organisations and enterprises which have outlived their usefulness. Nor is it always helpful to import indiscriminately what has been developed elsewhere.

Catholic action
20. Several decades ago lay people in many countries formed various kinds of apostolic movements and societies, in close liaison with the hierarchy of each country. Special mention must be made of those organisations which have been very effective, have been praised and promoted by popes and bishops, under the name of Catholic Action. They have often been described as a collaboration of the laity in the hierarchical apostolate.

Whether named or not, they do work of considerable value and have the following characteristics:

(a) Their objective is the same as the Church's: the evangelisation and sanctification of men and women and the Christian formation of their consciences, enabling them to imbue their environment with the Christian spirit.

(b) The laity contribute their experience and accept responsibility for directing these organisations, for investigating the conditions in which the Church's pastoral work is to be done and for the elaboration and execution of their plan of action.

(c) The laity act in unison and thus more effectively, offering a demonstration of the Church as community.

(d) The laity, whether acting on their own initiative or at the hierarchy's invitation, accept the hierarchy's direction. The hierarchy may also authorise the cooperation of the laity by explicit mandate.

Organisations which in the judgment of the hierarchy possess all these characteristics should be regarded as Catholic Action, whatever forms they may adopt or whatever names they have.

The Council commends these organisations. They certainly meet the Church's needs in many countries. It invites the priests and laity involved in them to develop more fully the characteristics listed above and always to cooperate with all other forms of the apostolate in the Church.

Special commendation

21. All apostolic organisations are to be esteemed. However, those which the hierarchy has praised, commended or founded in view of the needs of the times should be valued most by priests, religious and lay people and should be developed. Pride of place must go to international associations or societies of Catholics.

22. Especially praiseworthy are the lay people, married or single, who put their persons and their professional competence at the service of apostolic organisations. It is a great joy to see the number of lay people who do this in their countries

or abroad and especially on the foreign missions and the young churches.

Pastors should welcome such lay people with joy and gratitude. They will see to it that the requirements of justice, equity and charity are met in their regard and especially that they have sufficient resources for the maintenance of themselves and of their families. They should also be provided with the necessary training and with spiritual comfort and encouragement.

Chapter V

The order to be observed

23. The lay apostolate must be set in its true place within the apostolate of the entire Church. Union with those appointed by the Holy Spirit to rule the Church is essential, so also is collaboration among those engaged in the various apostolic enterprises, which it is for the hierarchy to systematise.

Mutual esteem and collaboration are essential for promoting the spirit of unity which will ensure that the Church's apostolate is marked by fraternal charity, that common aims are achieved and ruinous rivalries avoided.

This is most of all appropriate where a particular activity needs the agreement and apostolic cooperation of clergy, religious and laity.

Relations with the hierarchy
24. It is the hierarchy's duty to promote the lay apostolate, to provide it with principles and spiritual assistance, to direct its exercise towards the common good of the Church and to ensure that doctrine and order are safeguarded.

The apostolate permits different kinds of relationships with the hierarchy, depending on its forms and objectives.

There are many apostolic enterprises in the Church which lay people have initiated and which they run. They enable the Church, in certain circumstances, to fulfil its mission more effectively and are frequently commended by the hierarchy. No enterprise may claim the title "Catholic" if it lacks the approval of ecclesiastical authority.

Certain kinds of lay apostolate are, in various ways, explicitly recognised by the hierarchy.

Ecclesiastical authority may also choose to take under its wing and to accept responsibility for certain apostolic associations and enterprises, organising the apostolate differently if needs be, aligning it more closely with its own apostolic function, without however changing its specific nature or depriving the laity of their rightful freedom to act on their own initiative. Such an act of the hierarchy has been called a "mandate" in various ecclesiastical documents.

The hierarchy, finally, entrusts the laity with charges more closely related to the duties of pastors, such as the teaching of Christian doctrine, various liturgical actions and the care of souls. The laity are fully subject to higher ecclesiastical control in the discharge of these duties.

With regard to enterprises and institutions of the temporal order, it is for the hierarchy to teach and interpret the moral principles to be followed in this domain. It is also for it to judge whether such enterprises and institutions are in conformity with moral principles and to establish what is required in their regard for the safeguarding and promotion of the values of the supernatural order.

Relations with clergy and religious
25. Bishops and priests will remember that all the faithful have the right and duty to exercise the apostolate and that the laity have their part to play in building up the Church. They will therefore work as brothers with lay people in the Church and for the Church and will have a special concern for the laity and for their apostolic activity.

Priests with the ability and training for assisting special forms of the lay apostolate should be carefully chosen. They represent the hierarchy in this apostolic activity, promoting good relations between laity and hierarchy, fostering the spiritual life and the apostolic spirit of the associations confided to their care, offering them advice and encouragement. In constant dialogue with the laity they will search for ways of making their activity more fruitful, developing a spirit of unity within the association and between it and others.

Religious brothers and sisters will hold lay apostolic works in high esteem, will help to promote them, supporting, assisting and completing the work of the priests.

Special Councils
26. Councils should, where possible, be established in dioceses to assist the Church's apostolic work in evangelisation and sanctification, in charitable work, social relations and the rest, clergy and religious collaborating with the laity in whatever way is best. These councils can coordinate the various lay associations and enterprises, without prejudice to their autonomy.

Such councils should, where possible, be established at parochial, inter-parochial, diocesan, inter-diocesan, national and international levels also.

A special secretariat should be established at the Holy See for the service and promotion of the lay apostolate, supplying information about lay people's apostolic enterprises, undertaking research on problems in this domain and offering advice to hierarchy and laity. All lay apostolic movements and institutions should be represented in this secretariat and clerics and religious should be available to collaborate with the laity.

Cooperation with other christians and non-christians
27. Because of the gospel they share and with it the duty to bear a Christian witness it is desirable and often imperative that Catholics cooperate with other Christians in activities or in associations, at the individual level, the level of ecclesial communities and at national and international level.

Christians are sometimes required to work for apostolic ends with non-Christians who share human values with them.

Through such cooperation lay people bear witness to Christ the Saviour of the world and to the unity of the human family.

Chapter VI

Training for the apostolate

28. If the apostolate is to be fully effective training is required, not only because the lay person's spiritual and doctrinal progress demands it, but also because of the variety of circumstances, people and duties which he or she has to confront. This education must rest on the foundations expounded elsewhere by the Council (in the Constitution on the Church, chapters 2, 4 and 5). Some forms of the apostolate require special training.

Principles of training

29. Since lay people share in the Church's mission in their own way, they need an apostolic training which is in conformity with their lay state and spirituality.

Education for the lay apostolate presupposes an integral human education and proper integration into a person's own society and culture. It then involves in the first place learning to carry out the mission of Christ and the Church, living by faith in the divine mystery of creation and redemption, moved by the Holy Spirit to love God and humankind. This is the foundation of a fruitful apostolate.

As well as spiritual formation, solid grounding in doctrine is required: in theology, ethics and philosophy at least, in proportion to each one's capacity. A general culture linked with technical training is important.

Genuine human values are most important, especially the art of living and working on friendly terms with others and entering into dialogue with them.

Mere theoretical training is not enough. A person needs to learn to see all things and to judge and act in the light of faith, to improve himself or herself by working with others and thus to enter actively into the service of the Church. This education needs to be on-going, coupled with concern for the unity and integrity of the human person in order to preserve and intensify its harmony and equilibrium.

In this way, lay people insert themselves deeply into the heart of the temporal order and take their part in the world, at the same time making the Church present and active in it.

Those who train others for the apostolate

30. Training for the apostolate should begin at childhood, but it is especially important that adolescents and youths be initiated into the apostolate and imbued with its spirit, which training should be continued all through life. Christian educators have the duty of seeing to this apostolic education.

It is for parents to prepare their children from an early age to be aware of God's love for all men and women and to be concerned for their neighbour's spiritual and temporal needs. The family should be an apprenticeship to the apostolate.

Children should be taught to extend their interests to ecclesial and other communities. Involvement in the parish should make them aware of being members of the People of God. Priests, in performing their ministry, should be mindful of training for the apostolate.

Catholic educational institutions should foster an apostolic spirit in those in their care. Parents and those engaged in pastoral and apostolic activity have an even greater responsibility towards young people who do not receive an education in the apostolate because they do not attend Catholic schools or for whatever reason. Teachers practise an outstanding form of the lay apostolate and they need adequate learning and a thorough grasp of pedagogy if they are to achieve success in this branch of education.

Lay apostolic associations should concern themselves with education to the apostolate. It is often through them that such education is normally acquired. The members evaluate their methods and results and measure their behaviour by the gospel.

Training should take into account the entire range of the lay apostolate, for the lay apostolate is not limited to what takes places within a given association. All lay people should undertake their own preparation for the apostolate. This is especially true for adults as self-awareness grows and with it awareness of the range of achievements which their adult-hood makes possible.

Fields needing specialised training
31. Different types of apostolate require different types of training:

(a) The apostolate of evangelisation and sanctification: lay people should be specially trained for dialogue with believers and non-believers with the aim of taking Christ's message to all. But with the spread of materialism today, not only should they study Catholic doctrine, especially controverted points, they should confront materialism with the witness of evangelical life.

(b) Christian renewal of the temporal order: lay people should be instructed in the true meaning and value of temporal goods, both in themselves and in relation to the human person. They should gain experience in the right use of material things and in the organisation of institutions in the light of the common good and of the Church's moral and social teaching, in which latter they should be well versed.

(c) Works of charity and mercy testify to a Christian life and from their childhood the faithful should be taught to be concerned for those in need and to help them.

Aids to training
32. The faithful should avail of the many educational aids which are now available and which are adapted to the varying needs of the apostolate. There is need also for centres of research and documentation.

33. The Council appeals to the laity and especially to the younger generation to respond to the call of Christ and to make his interests their own as he sends them out into every town and every place as his cooperators, knowing that in the Lord their labour cannot be lost.